COMPLEX AMERICA

A Brief History of America's Breakdown (and God's Design)

Daniel L. Smith

Revealing Historical Truths Through First-Hand Accounts

PO Box 221974 Anchorage, Alaska 99522-1974

books@publicationconsultants.com, www.publicationconsultants.com

ISBN Number: 978-1-63747-041-1
eBook ISBN Number: 978-1-63747-042-8

Library of Congress Number: 2021942279

—First Edition—

Manufactured in the United States of America

I DEDICATE THIS BOOK TO EVERY SINGLE PERSON
STRIVING FOR TRUTH.
THE FACTS ARE HERE…
TODAY, YOU JUST HAVE TO LOOK A LITTLE HARDER.

Daniel L. Smith

FOREWORD

Have you ever read George Orwell's famous novel *1984*? How about *We* by Yevgeny Zamyatin? In Orwell's novel, society is running under an iron fist of authoritarianism. Much of the people are controlled by technology and brainwashed to support their governments dictatorship ideology. Of course the same fate happens in Zamyatin's *We* as well. Most people are hopelessly locked into what and how they are told to behave and remember by oppressive technology and evil government. Coincidently there are always one or two characters to the story who always seem to transcend the undeserving fate that humanity has fatally come to live by.

These two books are the most sought-after dystopian fictions in our modern history. Only time can be the judge of how society reacts to such thought-provoking reads. Why is it that you can only find a good dystopian novel located in the fiction section of your local bookstore? That is precisely why I decided to write *Complex America!* This book contains, not fiction, but a non-fiction pseudo-dystopian literature that is, in reality, what we know today as our *literal history.*

The information contained in this book is the type of historical evidence that has been buried—whether intentional or not--in the archival stacks for some time. The material in this book was selected and written out using a more personalized academic form of writing. While sticking to this format, I decided to seam the essays that I had authored together by personifying the literature. This method makes for easier understanding for all readers who a familiar with past and present historical events and current events.

The essays are ordered throughout this book by its historical relevance to occurrence. We start at Creation and move quickly through varying topics across the historical timeline. I culminate this literature with a Biblical Worldview. With the secularization (removing God) from public education in America, much of the information that opened up our knowledge to *why things had happened* has been filed away. Without freely clarifying these topical events to the general public—one should ask themselves—how would I have ever known?

This book is not meant to challenge the institutional establishment, nor is it meant to politically demean. This book is meant to explain, clarify, and present history *the way it actually happened.* I will attempt to give the reader a particular cause of an event and then I attempt to clarify the general effects afterwards. Hopefully, this will give the reader a better understanding of what had happened if they are not completely familiar with the general history of the topics contained herein. Again, this is not your typical history but a unique history of varying articles—from a Christian worldview.

Before you actually get into absorbing this information, know that these individual articles were written to personally relate in some way or fashion to current events. And ironically (because I wouldn't typically do that as a historian) this book is not presented in logical order. In not trying to confuse the reader, I split the information apart to shorten how much information is received. For the average person, the thick complexity of historical events and the amount of misinformation that's been fed to the American public; it only makes sense that I put a buffer in between the very real and very prominent history that has sewn our American fabric together. It would be way too overwhelming otherwise!

It is because of this that I have decided to keep this book to seamed articles, rather than writing a lengthy volume in covering a piece-by-piece history. Rather, it seems shorter histories seem to be appreciated much more in our modern-day age of instant gratification and lack of self-control. Ah! But I digress to say this: Assuming you went to public school and lived between 1960 and today—everything you read here will either, a.) teach you something new, or b.) re-inform you on what you have not been taught.

Either way, always remember what President Eisenhower stated to Congress in 1948: 'Those who do not learn history are doomed to repeat it."

Eisenhower wasn't talking about "made-up" history either…

Contents

The ARTICLES

THE MATRIX: WAKE UP & UNPLUG

What if I told you that everything you were taught since public school was a lie?

Maybe not *everything.* If you remembered your first lessons from history class, could you remember what they were about? If I took a wild guess, I would say that a lot of you all were taught that humanity arrived here over millions of evolutionary years. You were taught that by complete random chance, there was some perfect atomic cosmic equation that blasted the universe as we know it today into physical existence. Then you were probably taught that it was also the cavemen who evolved from primitive monkeys, who invented fire, and the stone-aged tools to adapt and survive. Did they also tell you that a large meteorite killed off all of the dinosaurs?

If you were taught any of these history lessons that I just mentioned, then congratulations! This realization was just the very start for detaching yourself from a very complex system of lies that has society outright clawing for direction, understanding, and divine hope. If I continued to insist on telling you that we have all been lied to on a massive scale, you might jump to the conclusion that I am a conspiracy theorist. While I am not one of those types, I certainly find differing theory's regarding historical and current-events quite interesting. It's because there will always be some form of natural truth to any theory. Discernment can be defined as the human ability to mentally determine the truth versus a lie.

And that's the main point to this article: *There is only one truth.*

In the 1998 hit sci-fi action film *The Matrix*, there was a scene in the movie that was a crossroad for the main character 'Neo.' Sitting in a black framed single chair, Neo, is completely enveloped in a white and quite vivid light. He almost struggles to keep up with his awareness. There is nothing that can be seen but this white, vivid, borderless room and Morpheus. Morpheus is an intellectual figure, clad in trench coat black with black mirrored frameless sunglasses. He circles Neo and asks him this: "I imagine that right now you're feeling a bit like Alice. Tumbling down the rabbit hole?"[1]

In the film, Neo works a corporate desk job and plays a low-key underground computer hacker by night for an extra buck. He lives completely unaware of the world around him and finds out his daily reality is a complete sham. He grasps an understanding of the "woke narrative" through the help of fellow insurgents that the system he "knows" is a total manipulation. Morpheus goes on

1 *The Matrix*. 1996. Film.

to say, "I can see it in your eyes. You have the look of a man who accepts what he sees because he's expecting to wake up. Ironically, this is not far from the truth. Do you believe in fate, Neo?" After responding back that he doesn't believe in fate, he tells Morpheus that he doesn't like the idea that he's not in control of his life.

THE LAND OF CONFUSION

Americans are in a state of confusion. Lack of true social direction, being inflamed by groups of powerful people looking to thrive politically inside of this said state of confusion. Young people today are frustrated with the inability to grasp onto the once triumphant American Dream. Generation gaps are creating confusion. Older generations of Americans are frustrated with the inability to grasp onto the lack of basic logic in this lightning-fast information-age. Social class is becoming all the more apparent, much reminiscent of the Middle Ages. Consequently this may have perhaps catapulted society and humanity into its final Revelation, much like the global war on terrorism, which has now become a cyclical institution to Americans. Presuppositions since the 1900's have been formed in America by poor efforts in education, lack of honest guidance, lack of political leadership, unhealthy entertainment saturated in most social and mainstream media platforms…all of this, combined with a complete lack of hope for the individual.

To understand our world thoroughly we need to grasp the concept that as human beings we start off with a fresh clean slate, comparable to that of a fresh hard drive on a computer. As we grow, our experiences and daily lessons both good and bad, shape out worldview. This is the way that we see and comprehend the world. This worldview, or presupposition, that we all obtain through daily life allows us to identify, relate to, and navigate life's future events. At one point in the early history United States of America—since our nation's conception actually—schooling was all done by way of all private means. Traditional homeschooling and church were the typical platforms you were taught under. These two systems would work together plurally *because* of the system of government design that America was founded upon. A family-oriented and Biblical education was at the core of our nation's early-academic success.

In the early 20th century public schools were secularized, meaning the government had all Christian fundamentals and its associated principles removed from the curriculum. Using an extremely slow social process of sociopolitical change called "Hegelian Dialect."

Yes, this is a real thing. Public schools, through progressive political leadership change over time, would slowly integrate Darwin's theory of evolution into the national curriculum along with Marx's social and secular leanings. The consequences would slowly erode God, Scripture, and Creation as some irrelevant religious dogma in the public school system. This process in turn "opened up" public school students to receiving false information, and thus causing a loss of foundational and fundamental direction in their own lives.

Pitfalls to Disenfranchised

It was essentially after the Civil War that Democrats had regained political power in most Southern states by the late 1870s. Later, this period came to be referred to as "Redemption". From 1890–1908, the Democrats and Republican radicals (which will now be called *radicals* for the rest of this article) passed statutes and amendments to their state constitutions that effectively disenfranchised most African Americans and tens of thousands of poor whites. They did this through devices such as poll taxes to vote and literacy tests to "qualify" (among other underhanded tactics). By the late 1950s, the Democratic Party again began to embrace the Civil Rights

Movement, and the old argument that Southern whites had to vote for Democrats to protect segregation grew weaker.

The Democratic party, in a post-Civil War & Reconstruction world, realized that regardless the outcomes of the Civil War and Reconstruction, the policy of "slavery-by-color" was over. Even segregation became an option not viable to their party's ethics, which is to oppress the poor regardless of color. So how did they do this? Well, modernization had brought factories, national businesses, and a more diverse culture to cities such as Atlanta, Dallas, Charlotte, and Houston. This attracted millions of northern migrants, including many African Americans.

They gave priority to modernization and economic growth over preservation of the"old ways" of the Democratic party. With the Southern economy being agricultural, and more recently industrial -- the Southern economy (owned by the majority Democratic elites) shifted their ideas towards a process of mass-manipulation which saturated the entirety of American culture. Over the years, from 1950 to the present day, the radicals have knowingly shifted their policy of slavery inward -- meaning slavery is now not just for people of color or of poverty, but all those people in our communities nationwide that are easily manipulated, fooled, or inherently ignorant.

The radicals shifted their focus to an emphasis on societal engineering that would ultimately program our society into being ego-driven, self-centered, ignorant, and constantly pushed by the liberal media. All of this only to chase a *never-to-arrive dream* of money, fame, and power. This new programming in our society started with television (ads & sitcoms) and its ability to woo over American society with mass-marketing. It's unnerving to think that the most vulnerable place to attack a person's psyche is their own home and place of comfort.

Scientists, psychologists, and technologists have all been part of this long-term planning -- knowingly and unknowingly. Radical leaders have set up institutions specifically aimed at buying up mainstream media outlets and funding universities for the benefit of pushing their political agenda and ethos. And in doing so they succeed in keeping the average family divided, damaged morally, and constantly in debt – complete social and financial slavery. This ultimately attacks one's own personal and fundamental direction in life. Slavery is still an invisible institution.

The consequential results for the individual? Loss of personal identity. Lack of proper information regarding the who, what, when, where, and why's in history and current events. And thus promoting a form of ignorance of historical facts. More than that though, it was the compounding effects of secular radio and mass-media on top of the unguided public school system that would amplify the detrimental psychological effects of schoolchildren. A peer of mine once wrote: "Cultivation theory, promoted by the late George Gerbner, argues that mass media, such as TV, cultivates in its audiences' fundamental assumptions and attitudes, which perpetuates the status quo, inhibiting social change that is outside institutionalized norms and practices."

Another Wake Up Call

President Lyndon B. Johnson (a Democrat) was a President whom I believed was the 1st President to come into the full knowledge of certain political shifts and the public's manipulation. The quote appeared for the first time anywhere on page 33 of Ronald Kessler's book, *Inside the White House: The Hidden Lives of the Modern Presidents and the Secrets of the World's Most Powerful Institution*, published in 1995: Johnson, like other presidents, would often reveal his true motivations in asides that the press never picked up. During one trip, Johnson was discussing his proposed civil rights bill with two governors.

Explaining why it was so important to him, he said it was simple: "I'll have them ni**ers voting Democratic for two hundred years." Further, "That was the reason he was pushing the bill," said MacMillan, who was present during the conversation. "Not because he wanted equality for everyone. It was strictly a political ploy for the Democratic party. He was phony from the word go." The "MacMillan" referenced above was Ronald M. MacMillan, a former Air Force One steward Kessler interviewed for Inside the White House.

This example illustrates today's radical establishment, which does not reflect the earlier Northern and Southern Democratic party of the early 19th century that carried moderate principles. It seems as though radical policies had been adjusted to remake the Democratic party of the 1860's. The political agenda of slavery has not stopped since abolition after the Civil War. enslaving an entirely different group of people; an ignorant people – siding with any entity that they can to achieve the means to the ends. This is not a political rant slamming the Democratic party, as much as it is a chronological and historical revelation to certain facts pertaining to our political and cultural origins. America has been fighting the same cultural battles since the Civil War; however, these battles are being fought in the much larger context of what is American culture.

Today's information received by the public is much more complex to grasp, and even harder than ever before to find an individual understanding of what "truth" actually means. I guess Phil Collins was right when his band Genesis made the music billboards in the late 1980's with their hit song "Land of Confusion." It was not just a play on American societal direction and what was to follow in the aftermath of the 1980's, but a seriously powerful and honest observation by a common man with a gift. Misleading the public is a serious pitfall with ramifications that will have serious consequences for our society.

Welcome to The Matrix

Back in the Matrix, Morpheus indifferent to Neo says: "I know exactly what you mean. Let me tell you why you're here. You're here because you know something. What you know, you can't explain. But you feel it. You felt it your entire life. That there's something wrong with the world. You don't know what it is, but it's there. Like a splinter in your mind -- driving you mad. It is this feeling that has brought you to me. Do you know what I'm talking about?"

Neo: "The Matrix?"

Morpheus: "Do you want to know what it is?"

The complete substance to the way that we see the world around us is further based on what we worship in our daily lives. For example, you spend countless hours neglecting your family for eyeballing stock-market trends, in hoping to make a quick investment for a quick-payout gamble. The resulting effects of worshiping the stock market can be extreme and unstable. Especially on your finances, on your career, and on your family. Your worldview? You see the world for its material assets and its benefits, and not for its logical ethical truths. This thought process will program an individual psychologically into a completely material way of viewing daily life and dealing with social interactions.

To reset how you view the world around you mean to reset your priorities in life. The first step, I suggest, is to understand and accept that God is the Creator of all things. As stated in Genesis. From the air that you breath, to the outer planets around us, to the fish in the sea, to the sun in the sky, He made his creation instantaneously. All things, even light and dark. In six days, His creation was complete, and He rested on the seventh. In His Creation, man was created in His image. Here humanity was born with Adam and Eve. This is the basic concept of history that must be understood by any one person if they want to have a fluid and complete understanding of our world around them.

Morpheus: "The Matrix is everywhere; it is all around us. Even now, in this very room. You can see it when you look out your window, or when you turn on your television. You can feel it when you go to work, or when you go to church or when you pay your taxes. It is the world that has been pulled over your eyes to blind you from the truth."

Neo: "What truth?"

Morpheus: "That you are a slave, Neo. Like everyone else, you were born into bondage, born inside a prison that you cannot smell, taste, or touch. A prison for your mind. (long pause, sighs) Unfortunately, no one can be told what the Matrix is. You have to see it for yourself. This is your last chance. After this, there is no turning back."

(In his left hand, Morpheus shows a blue pill.)

POLITICS & RELIGION: REALITY

I use education and academia as an example because it was the institutionalization of the public school system that opened up to mainstream secularist education that started in the early 20th century. It was during this time that the public school system was politicized for an agenda. This meant adjusting what was taught to children in schools. This included removing the original Christian principles in academia which included Biblically based morals, ethics, and a solid delivery system.in educational curriculum, then replacing it with purposeful misguided lies.

Here's the argument: If you could convince a child from an early age that human beings evolved from primates over millions of pointless years, you could convince the same child that there is no certainty to a true direction to life, thus enabling the ability to further misguide on true principles. To some extent you could continue to manipulate these children well into their early adulthood on false political pretenses. Such politics include politicians working with media moguls to keep people socially closed-up tight and blinded by their social-media and entertainment bubbles. These are intentional societal distractions meant to misguide, mislead, and make one stumble.

With a Christian worldview, or Biblical worldview, I must insist that it is the only foundational presupposition that logically incorporates both secular history and Scripture. In doing so, you receive the entire context of the world around you. This means that the "ability to reason from the Word of God and to relate its principles in every area of life was characteristic of the American" faithful prior to the American Revolution. Their election and sermons identified the principles of civil government with the principles of Christianity. Dr. Lawrence A Cremin in his study of American Education from 1607 to 1789, credits the high quality of American education to the Bible, "the single most important cultural influence in the lives of Anglo-Americans."

In our modern age, every generation of American born that has attended a typical public-school setting, has been born into an American system of secular indoctrination. This secularization has replaced God and Christian ethic with politically correct induced cultural tolerance and liberal ethic. A hard-wired secularist individual fresh out of graduation (if they made it that far) is now programmed for the public workforce, accountable only to man, government, and himself.

What this means is a consequential lack of social-control and the evaporation of solid leadership in our communities. I guess you could consider and contribute the lack of social control to many differing issues around the nation. Some could say there are many today who live in a real-life alternate reality through social-media and mainstream entertainment. This could be evidenced by their particular behaviors inside and outside public venues.

A NEW REALITY IN TRUTH

Morpheus: "You take the blue pill and the story ends. You wake in your bed and believe whatever you want to believe." (A red pill is shown in his other hand) "You take the red pill, and you stay in Wonderland and I show you how deep the rabbit-hole goes." (Long pause; Neo begins to reach for the red pill) "Remember -- all I am offering is the truth, nothing more."

(Neo takes the red pill and swallows it with a glass of water) It is your fundamental worldview that shapes your daily reality. I highly suggest and reiterate that it is only through Christianity, and through its ethical and moral frameworks that you will only be able to recognize and grasp onto what truth is. This includes an honest understanding of how the world works around us—in the past, in the present, and a completely educated observation of what lies ahead for everybody in the near future.

Welcome to the new post-Modern America. Nothing will be the same.

Hope in the Age of Confusion?

The United States of America was once a land squarely grounded in principles. That is, one fundamental philosophy and direction of movement as one united culture—of many cultures. What we encounter today, in our modern society, is a culture of many cultures and fundamental beliefs. With time comes mankind's natural urge to divide when critical historical social and political events take place in our nation.

In essence, it's like looking through a microscope starting with a group of cells. You would observe that when cells divide and split, they then form two new entities and multiply according to their same kind. A single cell divides to make two cells and these two cells then divide to make four cells, and so on. In professional science, this is called Mitosis or Meiosis. Parallel the Mitosis-effect with American history and you can see the similarities in how society naturally begins to breakdown with gradual change (a "Mitosis-like" change in thought – *see the next image*).

When you look at how the beginnings of America were established, you see that it all began as a small settlement with few people inspired by God's Liberty. We fast forward a few generations and you see that with population growth comes a majority and minority of how people think. Laws split, thinking splits, thus—society splits—enabling some confusion to some degree. But then, there is socially enabled confusion enabled by elites, corporations, and government.

Some could say it's a natural thing when debating what's truth and what's a lie. Some people appreciate how certain traditions are carried, others not so much. During the Age of Enlightenment and the Age of Discovery, you can see how liberal thought was distinguished completely differently than the liberal thought that we see today. One was aboutGod's Liberty for mankind, the other "liberty" is about "what can I do to gratify myself and my friends quickly."

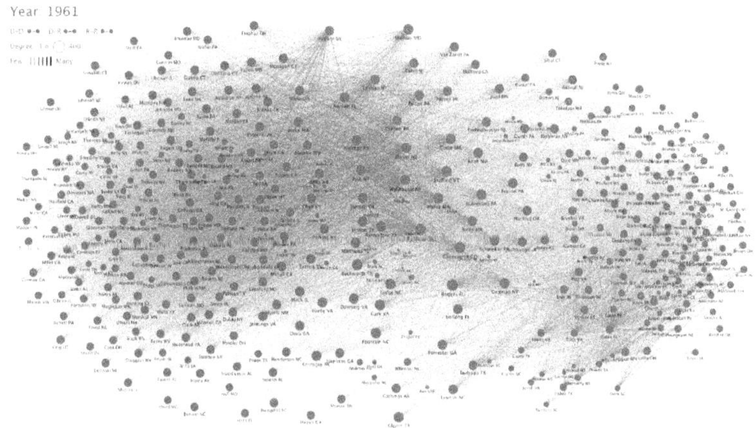

Here in America scales are tipping towards far-left liberalism as a societal "norm" and way of life. The problem with this is that there is no viability nor credibility in this lifestyle and thought. It keeps the greedy robbing the poor and the hurt wanting more and more to cover their private personal pain. So if the far-left Democratic leadership of this nation doesn't fit the frame of what is being discussed here, then how about those in elite positions that look to fix the narrative on typical American's attempting to live a normal life?

I digress here to point out that true Liberty is internal. The government cannot grant you internal liberty, nor can they take that away. The Founding Fathers of America, that is, the individuals that were propped up by God to found "a nation for all believers," – this was not some coincidence. It wasn't some deep-state draconian monarchial scheme to "keep the man down" either. On the contrary,God's Providenceis the grand overarching plan of how the world's narrative unfolds—and it rests squarely on *Him*. So let's break down the *very real* American principles laid out in the US Constitution.[2]

This information got my business account *banned from Facebook.*[3] You should check it out if you want to see the reality of it all. You see, the Bible and Civil Liberty are inseparable. There is no arguing this fact. EvenNewsweek, on December 26, 1982, *acknowledged* after a major analysis of the Bible's influence in America, that, "Now historians are discovering that the Bible, perhaps even more than the Constitution is our Founding document."[4]

"Dr. Donald Lutz, a professor of political science from the University of Houston, conductedexhaustive ten-year researchof about 15,000 political documents of the Founders' era (1760-1805), and recorded every quote or reference to another written source. This list of the 3,154 citations of the Founders was analyzed and published in Volume #78 of the American Political Science Review in 1983. The results would give quite an accurate measure of the influence of various sources of thought on the Constitution. The results were surprisingly contradictory to

2 "God's Providence in American History." Providence Foundation. Accessed May8,2021. https://providencefoundation.com/gods-providence-in-american-history/.

3 "Censored in 2020." Complex America | Daniel L. Smith | Historian & Author. Accessed May8,2021. https://www.complexamerica.org/censoredin2020.

4 "Newsweek December 27, 1982." Backissues.com - Back Issues of Magazines. Accessed May8,2021. https://backissues.com/issue/Newsweek-December-27-1982.

modern scholarship. By far, the most often quoted source of their political ideas was the Bible.[5]

This would account for over one-third (34%) of all their citations. Another 50% of all references can be attributed to authors who themselves derived their ideas from the Bible. Therefore, it can be said the 84% of the ideas in our Constitution are based directly or indirectly on the Bible." So it can be said that the fundamental principles all Americans would come live their lives by, was something they did based upon principle, whether they wanted to – knowingly or not.

Phil Collins, front man for 1980's band *Genesis*, would sing, "can't you see this is theland of confusion?"[6] The sad part is, the

5 Lutz, Donald S. "The Relative Influence of European Writers on Late Eighteenth-Century American Political Thought." *The American Political Science Review*78, no. 1 (1984): 189-97. Accessed May 8, 2021. doi:10.2307/1961257.

6 Genesis, "Land of Confusion." https://www.youtube.com/watch?v=Yq7FKO5DlV0.

'80s didn't do anything for American culture but push it farther into the trashcan. That's not an opinion, Mr. Collins was singing it, so you'll have to take it up with him. All jokes aside, if you thought America was the land of confusion then—today blows the 1980's out of the water.

We live in the Land of Confusion, in the Age of Confusion. Like it or not, it's not getting any better. There isno government that will be able to cure your problems.[7] There is no business that will be able to satisfy your instant gratification. There is no amount of money that will cure your moral and ethical ailments, and so, the same could be said about certain physical illnesses. In the Age of Confusion, that is, the age we currently live in—there is only one hope. Look up.

No matter what government is elected into office, no matter what laws are enacted or decreed, no matter how much stimulus money is shoveled out to The People--there will continue to be problems.[8] It will get worse. I reference theFall of Man, we as humankind are promised one ending to this entire history of the world.[9] It is not one that you can find in fiction either. It is but one book, the oldest literature in history, the Bible.

Regardless of your faith, there is only one reason America has been blessed so greatly. And in an era of time that has been unconditionally brutal towards its founding principles, it's critical to keep awareness to how we got here in the first place. Regardless

---

7 "The Government Doesn't Care About You." American Thinker. Accessed May8,2021. https://www.americanthinker.com/blog/2017/04/the_government_doesnt_care_about_you.html

8 "Survey: Americans Are The Unhappiest They've Been In Decades." WCCO | CBS Minnesota. Accessed May8,2021. https://minnesota.cbslocal.com/video/4598391-survey-americans-are-the-unhappiest-theyve-been-in-decades/.

9 "Was the Fall of Man a Good Thing?" Answers in Genesis. Accessed May8,2021. https://answersingenesis.org/sin/original-sin/fall-of-man-good-thing/.

of your place in society, we are all in this together. Not all the Founders were Christian, indeed, but nearly everybody knew who God the Father was (even tribal American Indians).[10] In the Age of Confusion, there is only one truth. The rest? Lies.

---

10 Smith, Daniel. *1845-1870 An Untold Story of Northern California: The American Settler's First Documented Accounts of their Unwelcome Arrival.* Publication Consultants, 2019. 44-45.

THE FRACTURE OF AMERICAN CULTURE

True American culture started where it was founded–right in the heart of the North American colonist at the run-up to the American Revolution. Of course over time that has all changed with quick population growth, cultural experiences, and historical events. And as with any cultural change comes a stark political and religious divide. It's a real thing that has the extreme potential for positive and negative outcomes. In the 1830s, in Brahmin Boston, Historian Perry Miller once observed, "there could hardly be found a group of young Americans number to the notion that there were any stirring implications in the word 'democracy.'"

Miller was right. Americans in the 1830s were, for the most part, were generally neutral in the way that American culture was beginning to shape out. There were ups and downs in our society. With a new nation and culture, life typically comes with nearly unlimited options on which direction to face the country–especially in regard to politics and culture. So where did our American breakdown begin? When did America go from "united as one" to completely polarized? It actually stems from a politically unconcluded Civil War in most cases. The Confederate (Democratic) leadership getting their full pardons from the consequences of treason and then reinstatement to government positions in 1865 may have started it all.

There was a hairline fracture that split the thinking of American traditionalists and progressive intellectuals. The Unitarian Church (a secular doctrine) was the catalyst, following transcendentalism in a close second. Traditionalists (such as the clergy and church) began to slowly halt providing leadership in our public schools and universities. Prior to this America lived under a purely Christian-based homeschooling education. This was the catalyst for America's rich culture and thorough economic success.

Harvard University (along with many others) was eventually taken over by the secular Unitarian church.[11] As the quality of public education began to decline, Horace Mann (the "father of progressive education") would convince the state of Massachusetts

11 "Harvard, Yale, Princeton, Oxford—Once Christian?" Answers in Genesis. Last modified June 27, 2007. https://answersingenesis.org/christianity/harvard-yale-princeton-oxford-once-christian/.

that the best way for education to grow would be to have the government take control, instead of the private sector (like families and churches).[12] What followed was *indoctrination* into a "self-culture," a humanistic thought process of "me, myself, and I" which enables individual materialistic behaviors.

Intersecting Politics and Religion

To break open a political divide for control and power, there must be a catalyst to enable a cultural shift. As a result, a false anti-Christian ideology of secular humanism was bred into American society. As traditional American doctrine became neglected, the competing ideology of socialism took off. Karl Marx's book, which was written in 1844, never had much influence in American society. That was until we completely backslid from traditional Christian principles of economics and dabbled in personal greed.

Resulting monopolies would form out of company buyouts and grow throughout our nation. One result of the Industrial Revolution was how wealth was accumulated instead of employing the extra resources to meet the actual needs of the poor and society. Self-culture and individual interest began to replace the common good of the American community. We were resultingly manipulated, so think of it as psychologically turning the lower and middle classes towards being arbitrary in daily ethics and morality.

In aninterview with Ravi Zachariasby Richard L. Schoonover, the associate editor of *Enrichment* journal, he mentions that "much of education in the 1960s came unhinged from any moral absolutes and ethical values to wit the book *Excellence Without a Soul* by Harry R. Lewis. We have seen this happening over the

12 "Horace Mann, Antichrist?" The New Republic. Last modified February 23, 2012. https://newrepublic.com/article/101048/horace-mann-antichrist.

last 40 years. There have been many voices alerting us to this. But more than just a philosophy took over; a mood took over."

"First, secularization generally held that religious ideas, institutions, and interpretations have lost their social significance. People liked the idea of a secular society and a secular government. But in terms of moral values and ethics, they never checked into the internal assumptions of secularization that made it wide open to almost any view on any subject. Beginning in the 1960s, the moods of secularization ultimately led to society's loss of shame."

"Next is pluralization, which sounds like a practical and worthy idea; and in many ways, it is. In pluralism, you have a competing number of worldviews that are available, and no worldview is dominant. But smuggled in with pluralization was the absolutization of relativism. The only thing we could be sure of was that all moral choices were relative and there was no point of reference to right and wrong. This resulted in the death of reason."[13]

So what happened to cause this major malfunction on such a mass scale? How did this cause a behavioral shift? What was the thought process behind this event? Well, why did the big screen hit film *Footloose* happen? Just kidding… but the behaviors portrayed in the film are a perfect example of the very real effects of our radically accelerated societal change.[14]

PLOT TO OVERTHROW TRADITION

Dr. Marshall Foster of the World History Institute writes that "in the loft restaurant above Peck's restaurant at 140 Fulton Street in lower Manhattan (building no longer stands), a group of young

13 "Interview: Ravi Z." Difficult Questions. Thoughtful Answers. | RZIM. Accessed May8,2021. https://www.rzim.org/read/just-thinking-magazine/defending-christianity-in-a-secular-culture.

14 "Footloose (1984)." IMDb. Last modified February 17, 1984. https://www.imdb.com/title/tt0087277/.

men met to plan the overthrow of the predominately Christian world-view that still pervaded America. At this first meeting, five men were present: Upton Sinclair, 27, a writer and a socialist; Jack London, writer; Thomas Wentworth Higginson, a Unitarian minister; J.G. Phelps Stokes, husband of a socialist leader; and Clarence Darrow, a lawyer."

"Their organization was called the Intercollegiate Socialist Society. Their purpose was to 'promote an intelligent interest in socialism among college men and women.' These men were ready to become the exponents of an idea passed on to them by an obscure writer named Karl Marx—a man who never tried to be self-supporting but was supported by a wealthy industrialist who, inexplicably, believed in his theory of 'the dictatorship of the proletariat.' Although a small group in the beginning, these adherents of socialism more than succeeded in their task."

"By using the proven method of gradualism, taken from the Roman general, Quintus Fabius Maximus, these men and others who joined with them slowly infiltrated' the public schools of our nation. By 1912 there were chapters in 44 colleges. By 1917 there were 61 chapters of student study groups of the League of Industrial Democracy. 'At that time John Dewey, the godfather of progressive education, was the vice-president of the league. By 1941 Dewey had become president and Reinhold Niebuhr, the liberal socialist theologian, was the treasurer."[15]

The beginning of the end of traditional America had become entrenched. Dr. Stephen K. McDowell, President of Providence Foundation, mentions in his book *America's Providential History* that "the loss of Christian tradition, character, and responsibility led to the failure of many banks in the early 1900s. To remedy

15 "America's Providential History (Including Biblical Principles of Education, Government, Politics, Economics, and Family Life)." Amazon.com. Accessed May8,2021. https://www.amazon.com/Providential-Including-Principles-Education-Government/dp/1887456007.

this situation, power was granted to a centralized Federal Reserve Board in 1913. But this unbiblical economic structure and lack of character produced many more problems. Within 20 years, the Stock Market had crashed, and America was in the midst of the Great Depression." With the propagation of socialism, people were ready for Roosevelt's New Deal, such as Social Security and other welfare agencies, which ultimately set up the State as a provider rather than God."[16]

A SUBTLE INDOCTRINATION

So here we are, nearing levels of socialism only seen in past welfare states. We, as one nation, are moving right on into 2021 at warp speed. It's an unknown future with no land in sight. The "land" that *we were* hoping for was one of principle, ethics, justice, responsible governing, and an honest commitment to *The People's* wants and needs. We haven't seen much of that fordecades by Congress.[17] With the arbitrary Biden-administration geared towards pure plurality and relativism, we may have furthercomplicated issuesto look forward to.[18]

At this point, maybe a tight chess match move, throwing the educational system into checkmate seems certainly appropriate? Too muchindoctrination has penetratedour culture.[19] What we have seen and have experienced today is the resulting violation of

16 Beliles & McDowell.

17 "Congress' Approval Drops to 18%, Trump's Steady at 41%." *Gallu p*. Last modified July 30, 2020. https://news.gallup.com/poll/316448/congress-approval-drops-trump-steady.aspx.

18 "Citing Rise of 'Christian Nationalism,' Secular Democrats Unveil Sweeping Recommendations for Biden." *Religion News Service*. Last modified December 1, 2020

19 McDowell, StephenK. "A Nation at Risk: Changing Textbooks Reveal the Secularization of American Education." Providence Foundation. Accessed May8,2021. https://providencefoundation.

our American values and traditions– all since the break of the 20th century. And it has all been done right under our distracted noses.

In closing, there has beena lot of chatterabout how Christians should stay out of politics… well, the entirety of The Bible is a sociopolitical history.[20] When Jesus Christ stood silent in front of the Pharisees in their court of justice–he was acting politically defiant in silence. Where do you think our *right to remain silent-* comes from in our Christian-American court of law? It's time for Christians to pro-actively be involved. Stop shying away from politics, especially when you are freely discussing it tonight at the dinner table.

---

com/a-nation-at-risk-changing-textbooks-reveal-the-seculariza-tion-of-american-education/.

20 Carter, Josh. "Christian Author Beth Moore Calls Trumpism Both 'seductive' and 'dangerous to the Saints of God'." Https://www.wlbt.com. Last modified December 14, 2020. https://www.wlbt.com/2020/12/14/christian-author-beth-moore-calls-trumpism-both-seductive-dangerous-saints-god/.

J. C. PENNEY: AN AMERICAN WITNESS TO GOD'S GRACE

American success starts with an idea, or philosophy. Any success in human existence starts with the same. However what many people seem to miss is that the core of any great idea, starts with God. In the Bible, the Book of Ecclesiastes was written by Solomon sometime around 931 BC. Ecclesiastes 12:13 says, "Let us hear the conclusion of the whole matter: Fear God and keep His commandment's, for this is man's all." Finally, Ecclesiastes 12

in summary concludes that the only value in life, is to live life from the perspective of God's endless economy. That is, the faithful perspective that God is omnipresent and in control over all things.

It is normal that each person searches for certain meanings and reasons in life. Everyone must build a foundation upon which they live their personal and daily lives. The author of Ecclesiastes, Solomon, would find out that worldly goals that do not lead towards God will only bring frustration, uncertainty, and disappointment. Enter here, Mr. James Cash Penney. This man would find out soon enough that Solomon was right on point.

J. C. Penney, through traditional hard-work and a careful lifestyle, would achieve success in building one of greatest retail companies in American history. In his biography it was written that from "inauspicious beginnings rose one of the great entrepreneurs in American history, a man with unusual dedication and exceptionally high ideals. James Cash Penney, Jr., was born September 16, 1875, near Hamilton, Missouri, to the Reverend James C. Penney and his wife, Fanny. The boy was one of twelve children, only six of whom survived to adulthood. His father was a less-than-prosperous Baptist preacher who also farmed."

"A man of strong Christian beliefs and upright morals, Reverend Penney raised his son with an abiding faith in God. The foundation of Penney's life was the Christian ethic of the Golden Rule, plus self-reliance, self-discipline, and a concept of personal honor. James Cash Penney climbed His way from humble beginnings to the top of the international retail market by an abiding practice of the name of His first store, The Golden Rule. In 1889 Penney took a small position in a dry goods store of the name The Golden Rule. Penney worked ambitiously and by 1902 He had impressed the owners into granting him a partnership. He opened His first Golden Rule department store on April 14, 1902 in Kemmerer, Wyoming."[21]

J. C. Penney looked for business "partners who could work as hard as he could while sharing his deep Christian values, which [for him personally] included complete abstinence from alcohol and tobacco."[22]Mr. Penney would bring his idea of retail stores across the Western Rockies, based upon Christian Ethic, or what is more commonly known today as the "Protestant Ethic." His ground-breaking ways of running shop would start by charging a flat price to all customers arriving to his stores, regardless of class and social standing. After making a couple smart business moves, Mr. Penney gained three more Golden Rule stores. Expansion would soon become a forefront of his business model.

In 1913, J.C. Penney would end up basing his retail operations out of Utah. Because of his entrance into the state as an "outsider," he was required by law to change the name of his company. And thus, what we know today as the J.C. Penney Co. was established. Going back to Mr. Penney's personal faith and ethic, he devised a plan to highlight the company's official slogan as, "Honor, Confidence, Service, and Cooperation."[23]

Showing his Christian values firsthand, Mr. Penney founded the J. C. Penney Foundation in 1925. He would go on to assist groups such as adoption programs, homeless shelters, youth organizations, vocational schools, libraries, family counseling centers, missions and missionary programs, and health clinics (among others). He would also go on to build a 120k-acre farming community in northern Florida. There, poor and needy individuals could arrive to work, farm, and rebuild their livelihoods. Mr. Penney would

---

21 Penney, JamesC. *J.C. Penney: the Man with a Thousand Partners: An Autobiography of J.C. Penney*. 1931.

22 Kruger, David Delbert. 2012. "Earl Corder Sams and the Rise of J. C. Penney."*Kansas History* 35 (3): 164–85.

23 Penney.

even go on to build a 60-acre Memorial Home Community, where retired pastors/ministers, church volunteers and works, missionaries, and their entire families could live in peace.

It was during the Great Depression of the 1930's that Mr. Penney would experience extreme financial hardships. This in turn would lead to significant stress, which would transform into a life-threatening sickness. While he was in the hospital, his wife and son would receive many "goodbye" letters, written in sadness. The next morning, Mr. Penney would awake and go for a walk down the hospital hallway. As he walked, he heard a faint singing, which grew louder as he continued.

Mr. Penney would arrive at the hospital chapel, where he would walk inside and listen to hymns and psalms with a sad heart. It was the song, "God Will Take Care of You" that had punctually put hope into his soul. Soon after, in a life-transforming instant, Penney was saved and changed. He had discovered that God was there to help him. He would take these Christian principles with him into the business world.

According to James Cash Penney himself, the company slogan of "Honor, Confidence, Service, and Cooperation," was officially applied to the company philosophy, doctrine, and mission as a daily routine. In the end, he would go public with the J. C. Penney Company. He would give all managers share of the company stock and would later also include all associates in corporate profit-sharing. This was generous for the typical American corporation.[24]

By 1971, J.C. Penney had 1660 stores in North America. He was quoted as saying, "From that day to this, my life has been free from worry."[25]It was in the face of circumstances that could have meant a physical death, it was J. C. Penney, right there next to Solomon the author of Ecclesiastes. He also found a new life. He would find the most foundational answer to all of life—God's unconditional love.

The rest is history...

---

24 Penney.

25 Lee, Richard. "Ecclesiastes." In The American Patriot's Bible, NKJV. Nashville: Thomas Nelson Publishers, 2012.

Apollo 8, Genesis, and Faith

In History, the Bible is considered both a primary and secondary historical source.[26] There are two reasons for this. First, since most of the Old Testament was documented by one man—Moses, as a recollection under the inspiration of God—we then consider this text a secondary historical source. Of course there were other authors to the Old Testament, but a great main example. Second, the New Testament is documented by multiple men from first-hand accounts. This means, they were there. They saw and experienced the events taking place at the time. Thus, they recorded it on paper. This means that each book written in the second part of the Bible was written down as a witness to daily historical events.

Let us consider Genesis, as it was said "In the Beginning," was the first book of the Bible written by Moses. This man, who physically spoke with God, lived for hundreds of years.

26 Goswell, Gregory. "The Two Testaments as Covenant Documents." Journal of the Evangelical Theological Society 62, no. 4 (December 2019): 677–92.

Written around 1440 BC, Moses would be the first to write the history of humanity under the divine inspiration of God. Foundations, or principles, are critical to the success of any project. This goes from crafting a house to crafting an entire nation. When the Founding Fathers of set out to create the cement slab that would define America's greatness, they went right to the source of that greatness. They would openly declare all human beings are "endowed by their Creator with certain unalienable Rights…"[27]

Genesis holds the principle foundation of truth that God is the source of all things and our only hope for true peace, happiness, and liberty that each of us crave inside. Genesis is the "book of beginnings," and through its text we see God's divine crafting of heaven and earth through His Word. We witness Man's rebellion and sin; we also see God's calling on a covenant with the very people through which He would bring salvation and redemption. Gods saving grace would be given to the people of the earth through His one and only Son.

Genesis is the description of how the universe, the earth, and creation were made. We can look up on any given night to see God's craftmanship with our own eyes. Each star and planet pinned in place with perfection. His artwork is accentuated by the asteroids, nebulas, and supernovas that expand the vastness of space. Even when tuned into the sounds of space, you would hear a rhythmic pattern of energy. That right there is what could be called evidence, or one big clue.

Pastor Louie Giglio proved this on one of his sermons recorded during a live presentation.[28] So what we see here is certain evidence that all life is connected through God, the Creator. With the Bible being the infallible Word of God—this proof becomes even more foundational.

America's first manned mission to circle the moon would be completed on Christmas Eve, 1968. That evening, the three astronauts—Jim Lovell, William Anders, and Frank Borman—would film a live-television presentation during the 9th lunar orbit.

---

27 "Declaration of Independence: A Transcription." National Archives. Last modified May 29, 2020.https://www.archives.gov/founding-docs/declaration-transcript.

28 *Symphony*. Directed by Louie Giglio. 2012. Film. https://www.godtube.com/watch/?v=F20CFCNU

During this time they would show the nation pictures of the Moon and Earth as seen from the Apollo 8 space craft. For the late 1960's this event was the most watched television broadcast in history.[29]

What people do not know is that nearly six-weeks prior to the shuttle launch, a NASA official had called Astronaut Frank Borman with a special request, "We figure more people will be listening to your voice than that of any man in history. So we

29 "Apollo 8 astronaut marks 1968 broadcast to Earth." *Daily Herald [Arlington Heights, IL]* 24 Dec. 2013: 9. *Business Insights:Global.* Web. 10 Mar. 2021.

want you to say something appropriate."[30] At the end of the live broadcast, the three-man team of Apollo 8 took turns reading passages from the Book of Genesis:

William Anders:"We are now approaching lunar sunrise and, for all the people back on Earth, the crew of Apollo 8 has a message that we would like to send to you. 'In the beginning God created the heavens and the earth. And the earth was without form, and void: and darkness was upon the face of the deep. And the Spirit of God moved upon the face of the waters. And God said, Let there be light: and there was light. And God saw the light, that it was good: and God divided the light from the darkness.'

Jim Lovell:"God called the light Day, and the darkness He called Night. So the evening and the morning were the first day. Then God said, 'Let there be a firmament in the midst of the waters, and let it divide the waters from the waters.' And God made the firmament and divided the waters which were under the firmament from the waters which were above the firmament; and it was so. And God called the firmament Heaven. So the evening and the morning were the second day."

Frank Borman:"Then God said, 'Let the waters under the heavens be gathered together into one place, and let the dry land appear'; and it was so. And God called the dry land Earth, and the gathering together of the waters He called Seas. And God saw that it was good.' And from the crew of Apollo 8, we close with good night, good luck, a Merry Christmas—and God bless all of you, all of you on the good Earth."

---

30 Borman, Frank, and RobertJ. Serling. *Countdown: An Autobiography*, 194-195. 1988.https://archive.org/details/countdownautobio0000borm/mode/2up

THE BOOK OF ROMANS AND AMERICAN PRINCIPLE

One of my all-time favorite books of the Holy Bible is Romans. There are a few reasons I say this. My most common explanation for this, is the parallel to our current day and age. The United States of America has begun to fall the same fate as the ancient Roman Empire. This isn't a myth. History is the fabric of actual national and regional events occurring daily. This is what makes antiquity, or what is called the past. As with humanity, the world is a fallen place.

The Roman Empire may have been a historical foreshadowing of what America later aimed to be in material glory. The end results for all parties involved though are the same. Rome, as with America, existed for itself. The life of a Roman was existence to the State. It was conforming to what society said was acceptable, which again, appears much like American society in our modern era. If the Judeo-Christian principles that were first established by the Founding Fathers are abandoned, then what better are we than the Romans? We are not.

Three things begin to happen to people once they begin conforming to what society tells them to be. Stagnation, rebellion, and then finally, collapse. So let's say you watch the evening news, a news segment ends and a commercial pops up. Flashy stuff, huh? The problem here is that marketing media moguls force onto the consumer (of cable television and mass media) their vision of how society should act and look. With education being watered down, it's to no surprise that the abandonment of the Founding Christian ideas has become more forefront.

Prior to the educational system being messed with at the break of the 1900's, Christianity was commonplace. It was considered normal to attend church, study scripture, and support your neighbor in their daily affairs. In fact, church at one time was the only place you could receive your political news. It is this fact that evidences the inseparability of church and state function. America was designed into the fabric of its culture Judeo-Christian values. Without them, we are Romans. Without them, we are broken. Without them, we will not stand as one Nation under God, indivisible, with liberty and justice for all. After all, are we not the Roman Empire?

Paul the Apostle wrote the Book of Romans around 57 A.D. The theme of Paul's book was The Righteousness of God. One key verse states: "For I am not ashamed of the Gospel of Christ, for it is the Power of God to salvation for everyone who believes, for the Jew first and also for the Greek. For in it the righteousness of God is revealed from faith to faith; as it is written, "The just shall live by faith." – Romans 1:16-17. Chapters six through eight contain the foundational principles on the spiritual life. Romans' answers questions on how to be delivered from a sinful life, and instead show how to live a balanced lifestyle through grace, and through the power of the Holy Spirit.

Romans dives deep into the critical importance of Jesus Christ's sacrificial death on the cross at Calvary. Paul, using a question-and-answer format, prepares the most systematic presentation of doctrine in the Bible and balances his narrative with practical encouragement. With undivided application of Scripture to the daily lifestyle of the Christian believer results in a life being lived in righteousness. This virtue is reflective of the open grace of God.

In 1911, President Woodrow Wilson gave delivered a famous speech in Denver, Colorado. His speech was called, "The Bible and Progress." In his speech Wilson told the crowd, "America was born a Christian nation. America was born to exemplify that devotion to the elements of righteousness which are derived from the revelations of Holy Scripture." It was out of this foundational thought, this principle, which laid out the Declaration of Independence and the US Constitution. It is America that promises us a life to be lived in virtue. In 1976, President Jimmy Carter said, "We have a responsibility to try to shape government so that it does exemplify the will of God."

THE ARTICLES OF DIS-INTEGRATION (AND EDUCATION)

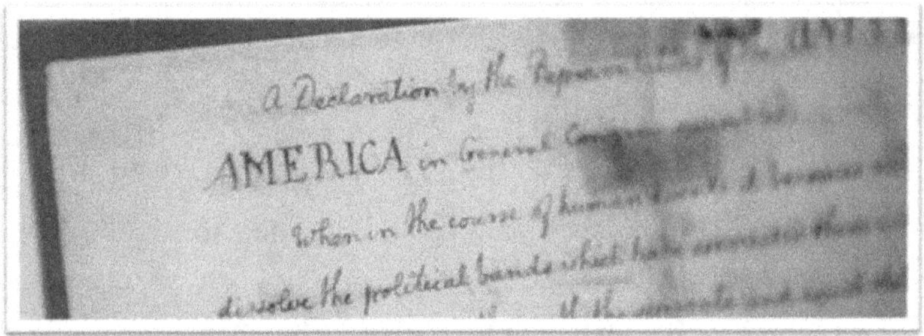

When I investigate societal breaks, I investigate morals, ethics, and presumptions. I also investigate cultural varieties and similarities through behavioral and customary tendencies. With that all being said, I am aware of a break in traditional (what was once known as normal) academic thinking at the break of the 20th century. This thinking spilled over into political discourse. Of course, this whole phenomena started well before that. I wrote about it in an earlier article recently where I mentioned that therewas a hairline fracture that split the thinking of American traditionalists and progressive intellectuals.

In the 19th going into the 20th century, the Unitarian Church (a secular "church") was the catalyst. Traditionalists (such as the clergy and church) began to slowly halt providing leadership in our public schools and university's (prior to this was a purely homeschooling education). Harvard was taken over by the Unitarian church, and as the quality of public education began to decline, Horace Mann (the "father of progressive education") would convince the state of Massachusetts that the best way for education to grow would be to have the government take control, instead of the private sector (like families and churches).[31] Fast forward to our Modern era. With the propagation of socialism, people were ready for Roosevelt's "New Deal," such as Social Security and other welfare agencies, which ultimately set up the State as provider rather than God.

It was exactly this break in thinking that brought back certain negative concepts of "race." This time however contemporary and glorified in other ways geared towards bending one's political thought or will towards the leftist ideology, saturating into any historical topic. Our history, as of the break of the 20th century, has been manipulated to make certain academic agenda's fit the needs to a political end as mentioned before. A great example is the evidence in our academic texts over the course of this time.

Professor Paul C. Vitz in a government funded study he conducted in the 1980s on whether bias exists in public school textbooks. His study clearly showed bias, and censorship exists, and the nature of the bias is clear: "*Religion, traditional family values, and conservative political and economic positions have been reliably excluded from children's textbooks.*"[32]

---

31 Beliles, Mark A., and Stephen K. McDowell.*America's Providential History: Including Biblical Principles of Education, Government, Politics, Economics, and Family Life*, 253. 1989.

32 Paul C. Vitz,*Censorship, Evidence of Bias in Our Children's Textbooks*, Ann Arbor, Mich.: Servant Books, 1986, p. 1.

Vitz wrote that while the bias may not be deliberate, a "secular and liberal mindset appears to be responsible." And he points out that the bias is primarily manifested by exclusion. As an example, "sixty representative social studies textbooks were carefully evaluated" and "none of the books covering grades 1 through 4 contain one word referring to any religious activity in contemporary American life." While these social studies texts mention the family, "the idea that marriage is the origin and foundation of the family is never presented. The words marriage, wedding, husband, wife, do not occur once in these books."[33] It is not surprising why so many Americans today reject the biblical view of the world (let alone history and family).

An excerpt from McDowell of Providence Foundation mentions:

The social studies texts frequently presented 'role models' but 'not one contemporary role model is conservative and male.' High school U.S. history texts almost completely ignored major religious events of the past 200 years and there was "constant omission of reference to the large role that religion has always played in American life.' This was true for elementary texts as well. In one second grade history book, 30 pages were given to the Pilgrims, but they were "described entirely without any reference to religion." At the end of the first year they observed a day of Thanksgiving, but no mention is made of the fact that they gave thanks to God.

Christian bias via exclusion continues in current textbooks. For example, one recent history text quotes the Mayflower Compact: 'We whose names are under-written … do by these presents solemnly and mutually in the presence of God, and one of another, covenant and combine our selves together into a civil body politick.' What was omitted from this important historical document? Their clear Christian motive: "*for the glory of God, and advancement*

33 Vitz, 1.

of the Christian faith and honor of our king and country, a voyage to plant the first colonie in the Northern parts of Virginia."

Bias is not only expressed by exclusion but also by changing the meaning of a text or writing. One U.S. History Advanced Placement textbook summarizes the Second Amendment as, "The people have the right to keep and bear arms in a state militia," which is an inaccurate meaning of the amendment which clearly states, "the right of the people to keep and bear arms shall not be infringed." This same text says the First Amendment gives us a "separation of church and state," failing to explain this amendment does not separate God from government or religious ideas from public life. Rather, it acknowledges a jurisdictional separation between the institution of civil government and the institution of the church.

Misrepresenting motives is another means of bias. Under the heading 'Roots of American Government,' a popular seventh-grade Houghton Mifflin Social Studies textbook expounds: 'Enlightenment thinkers in the American Colonies were excited. Here they were, the first people in history to have the chance to create an entirely new government based on Enlightenment Principles.' However, America was not created by Enlightenment thinkers on Enlightenment ideas, but according to John Adams, the general principles on which the fathers achieved independence were … the general principles of Christianity.'

(…) Some texts teach direct lies, like a high school history textbook published by Pearson that teaches Trump is mentally ill and his supporters are racists. In other texts the Founders of America are often presented as atheists, agnostics, or secularists who wanted no religious influence in public life, when in fact, all but a couple of the Signers of the Declaration and two or three members of the Constitutional Convention were orthodox

Christians who believed the foundation of free nations rests on the Christian faith."[34]

It is the above-mentioned analysis on education that feeds into the most common misconceptions and errors; of replacing traditional thought and history which was considered normal daily prior to 1900. I feel this is the most harmful to developing an accurate history and historical interpretation of the early American encounters upon which the course has focused. But of course this is just one point of many out there.

34 McDowell, Stephen K. "A Nation at Risk: Changing Textbooks Reveal the Secularization of American Education." Providence Foundation. Accessed February 13, 2021.https://providencefoundation.com/a-nation-at-risk-changing-textbooks-reveal-the-secularization-of-american-education/.

The Desiderata and Old St. Paul's Church, 1692

Many people have found hope in these words. Many people have also been misled.

St. Paul's Church mentions "legend has it that the Desiderata was inscribed on a wall at Old St. Paul's Church in the late 17th century. In reality, it was written in 1927 by Max Ehrman, an Indiana attorney, poet, and author. Old St. Paul's is in no way accountable for the poem."

Desiderata and Old St. Paul's "Go placidly amid the noise and haste and remember what peace there may be in silence." So begins the popular poem known as Desiderata, which has comforted and inspired millions of people throughout the world. Known for its words of reassurance, Desiderata has been reprinted in national magazines such as Reader's Digest, been recited at countless weddings and funerals, and was recorded as a hit pop song in 1972. Over the years, the source of this well-loved poem has been shrouded in mystery.

Legend has it that the Desiderata was inscribed on a wall at Old St. Paul's Church in the late 17th century. In reality, it was written in 1927 by Max Ehrman, an Indiana attorney, poet, and author. Old St. Paul's is in no way accountable for the poem.

So how did Desiderata become associated with Old St. Paul's? To find the answer we must trace back to the season of Lent in Baltimore in the mid 1950's. The Reverend Frederick W. Kates, rector of Old St. Paul's from 1956 to 1961, plays a key role in this story. During Lent it was Father Kates' custom to distribute inspirational poems and quotations to his parishioners. One particular Sunday he placed Desiderata in the pews on parish letterhead, which contained the church's founding date of 1692.

One can only surmise a visitor then copied the poem, along with the misleading credit line, and distribution began in earnest. Even today it is rare to find a copy of Desiderata that fails to include the line "Found in Old St. Paul's Church, Baltimore, Dated 1692." The parish has received inquiries on this piece of poetry from every state in the Union and from countries throughout the world. Desiderata's popularity endures and so does its mistaken association with Old St. Paul's.

This excerpt is taken directly from a publication made directly from Old St. Paul's Church:

"Go placidly amid the noise and the haste and remember what peace there may be in silence. As far as possible, without surrender, be on good terms with all persons. Speak your truth quietly and clearly; and listen to others, even to the dull and the ignorant; they too have their story. Avoid loud and aggressive persons; they are vexatious to the spirit. If you compare yourself with others, you may become vain or bitter, for always there will be greater and lesser persons than yourself."

"Enjoy your achievements as well as your plans. Keep interested in your own career, however humble; it is a real possession in the changing fortunes of time. Exercise caution in your business affairs, for the world is full of trickery. But let this not blind you to what virtue there is; many persons strive for high ideals, and everywhere life is full of heroism. Be yourself. Especially do not feign affection. Neither be cynical about love, for in the face

DESIDERATA

GO PLACIDLY amid the noise and the haste, and remember what peace there may be in silence... As far as possible, without surrender, be on good terms with all persons. Speak your truth quietly and clearly; and listen to others, even to the dull and the ignorant; they too have their story. Avoid loud and aggressive persons; they are vexatious to the spirit... If you compare yourself with others, you may become bitter or vain, for always there will be greater and lesser persons than yourself. Enjoy your achievements as well as your plans. Keep interested in your own career, however humble; it is a real possession in the changing fortunes of time... Exercise caution in your business affairs, for the world is full of trickery. But let this not blind you to what virtue there is; many persons strive for high ideals, and everywhere life is full of heroism... Be yourself. Especially do not feign affection. Neither be cynical about love; for in the face of all aridity and disenchantment, it is as perennial as the grass... Take kindly the counsel of the years, gracefully surrendering the things of youth. Nurture strength of spirit to shield you in sudden misfortune. But do not distress yourself with dark imaginings. Many fears are born of fatigue and loneliness. Beyond a wholesome discipline, be gentle with yourself. You are a child of the universe no less than the trees and the stars; you have a right to be here. And whether or not it is clear to you, no doubt the universe is unfolding as it should. Therefore be at peace with God, whatever you conceive Him to be... And whatever your labors and aspirations, in the noisy confusion of life, keep peace in your soul. With all its sham, drudgery and broken dreams, it is still a beautiful world. Be cheerful. Strive to be happy.

Max Ehrmann

of all aridity and disenchantment, it is as perennial as the grass. Take kindly the counsel of the years, gracefully surrendering the things of youth. Nurture strength of spirit to shield you in sudden misfortune."

"But do not distress yourself with dark imaginings. Many fears are born of fatigue and loneliness. Beyond a wholesome discipline, be gentle with yourself. You are a child of the universe no less than the trees and the stars; you have a right to be here. And whether or not it is clear to you, no doubt the universe is unfolding as it should. Therefore be at peace with God, whatever you conceive Him to be. And whatever your labors and aspirations, in the noisy confusion of life, keep peace in your soul. With all its sham, drudgery, and broken dreams, it is still a beautiful world. Be cheerful. Strive to be happy."

THE ROOTS OF OUR LIBERTY

"My only hope of salvation is the infinite, transcendent love of God manifested to the world by the death of His Son upon the cross. Nothing but His blood will wash away my sins. I rely exclusively upon it. Come, Lord Jesus! Come quickly!" – Benjamin Rush, Signer of the Declaration of Independence.

"The general principles upon which the Fathers achieved independence were the general principles of Christianity are as eternal and

immutable as the existence and attributes of God." – John Adams, Second President of the United States.

"He who made all men hath made the truths necessary to human happiness obvious to all... Our forefathers opened the Bible to all."– Samuel Adams, Signer of the Declaration of Independence.

Over the course of the last decade or so, many people have attempted to dismiss the fact that America was founded upon the Biblical principles of Judeo-Christianity, all the attempts in the world to revise history will never, ever, change the facts. Those who take the time to examine the original writings, diaries, personal letters, biographies, and publicly made statements, would be shocked to quickly recognize the Christian worldview behind the individuals who were instrumental in planting the Christian-American roots of liberty. In further looking into the writings and biographies of these individuals, you will see a heavy-handed use of quotes. These quotes evidence the reach of how the Christian worldview would influence their daily thinking and lives.

So, here's the stump in the road. Arguments of how not all the Founding Fathers were Christian have been common, and it's true. It is clear that not all were followers of Christ. The point here is that even those who were not of the faith *were completely influenced* by the principles of Christianity. It is this fundamental mind-set that allowed for the shaping of America's political ideas. It really becomes possible to become so distracted with whether individuals such as Thomas Jefferson or Ben Franklin put their personal faith in Jesus Christ, that one completely misses the fact that the Founders all thought from the Biblical worldview, that is, the Christian lens—whether they believed it or not.

The overall Christian consensus in colonial America helped to shape the Founders views and thinking when writing the founding documents and nations laws. This all resulted in the Republic that we all live in today. Here, the Declaration of Independence was specific in identifying the source of all authority, and rights, as "Their Creator," and then emphasized on the that individual human rights were God-given and not man-made. As a result, there would be no king, queen, or emperor, nor would there be just one established state religion. Because of this simple direction, there would be no tyrant to stand in the way of human liberty---or self-respect, which are uniquely Judeo-Christian.

Most historians do not consider the "Founding Fathers" to the fifty-five delegates to the Constitutional Convention, this core-group of individuals painted a picture of the Christian sentiments of those who shaped the political roots of America. So let's investigate the matter of public record here. The delegates included:

28 Episcopalians, 8 Presbyterians, 7 Congregationalists, 2 Lutherans, 2 Dutch Reformed, 2 Methodists, 2 Roman Catholics, 1 Unknown, and 3 Deists (Deists believe that God is impersonal and left earth to man to run its course). So, a whopping 93% were members of the Christian church and 100% of them were completely influenced by the Biblical worldview of government and humanity.

In just a brief study of the Founding Fathers last wills and testaments, you should be convinced that their own personal declarations were backed by strong Biblical beliefs. Now add to that their personal accounts concerning their utmost faith in Jesus Christ. Throw in their roles in leadership, the guiding of many Bible societies, their participation in ministry… the evidence is overwhelming.

A Justification for the Nation of Israel

Over time there have been many questions into why the United States of America even supports Israel and its political interests in the first place. Many Americans today cast Israel aside without thinking twice about the world's first true God-given nation. Just recently, a man who was speaking publicly in Washington DC mentioned, "God created Israel because he loved man, man created America because they [man] loved God." There is a reason that this was stated, and it's because of where the history lies.

THE TWELVE TRIBES OF ISRAEL
Around 1200-1050 B.C.
(according to the Book of Joshua)
Mediterranean Sea
Sidon
Tyre
ARAMEANS
Ijon
Dan
ASHER
NAPHTALI
Kedesh
Hazor
Chinnereth
Ashteroth
Hamath
BASAN
ZEBULUN
ISSACHAR
Edrei
Dor
Megiddo
Jezreel
Camon
Taanach
Bethshean
Ramoth-Gilead
MANASSEH
Tirzah
Shamir
Shechem
Zaphon
Mahanaim
Pirathon
River Jordan
Aphek
Shiloh
Joppa
DAN
EPHRAIM
GAD
AMMON
Bethel
Gilgal
Jazer
Rabbath Ammon
Gezer
Gibeon
Jericho
Ekron
BENJAMIN
Jerusalem
Heshbon
Mephaath
Ashdod
Bezer
Mount Nebo
Bethlehem
Ashkelon
Gath
Jarmuth
REUBEN
PHILISTIA
Lachish
JUDAH
Jahaza
Gaza
Hebron
Debir
Eshtemoa
Dead Sea
Gerar
Beersheba
Arad
MOAB
SIMEON
Kirhareseth
AMALEK
Zoar
Wilderness of Zin
EDOM
Tamar
Zalmona
Bozrah
Kadesh
Punon

Call it organic history. It's a rich history. It's a national history so deep, that it's in the Bible. It's a nation however that's been actively slandered by many who are very unaware of the past--both ancient and recent. This is the resulting thought process of secularized history. Is it unreasonable to believe Christianity being in rapid decline for the last 60 years parallel the lack of support for Israel? Yes, it sure does. And there really is an honest answer behind this whole Israeli American international relationship. As the Bible mentions, it was political boundaries that were established here--before any other nation on earth.

First, look here at the original Twelve Tribes of Israel:

Now, look at the current map of Israel today:

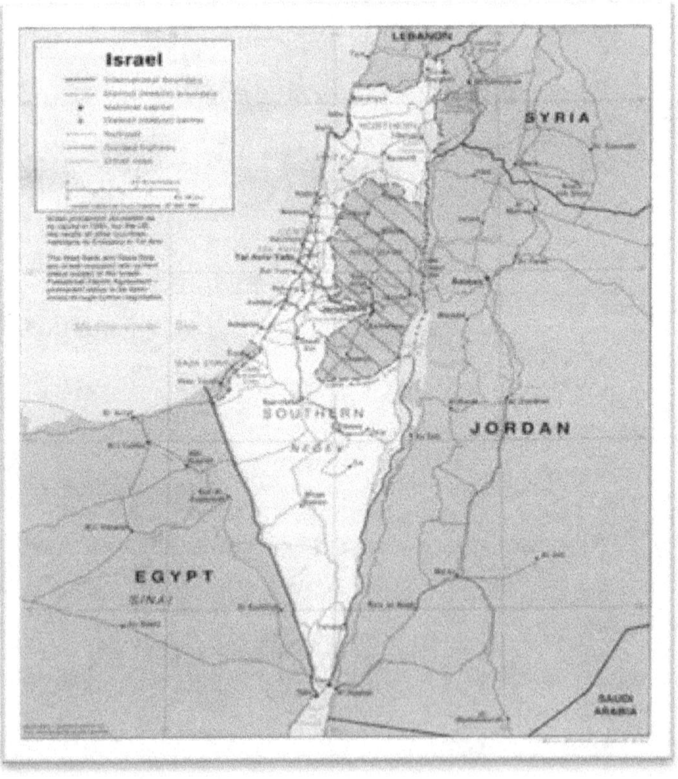

Over time, Persia would end up establishing its massive Dynasty and the later, Alexander the Great of Macedonia (Greece), would take a bite out of Persia's strategy in overall dominance and influence. Wars have always been fought since the Fall of Man (read Genesis). When wars occur, boundaries change. Let's look at the history here as evidenced by maps over time.

First look at Ancient Persia:

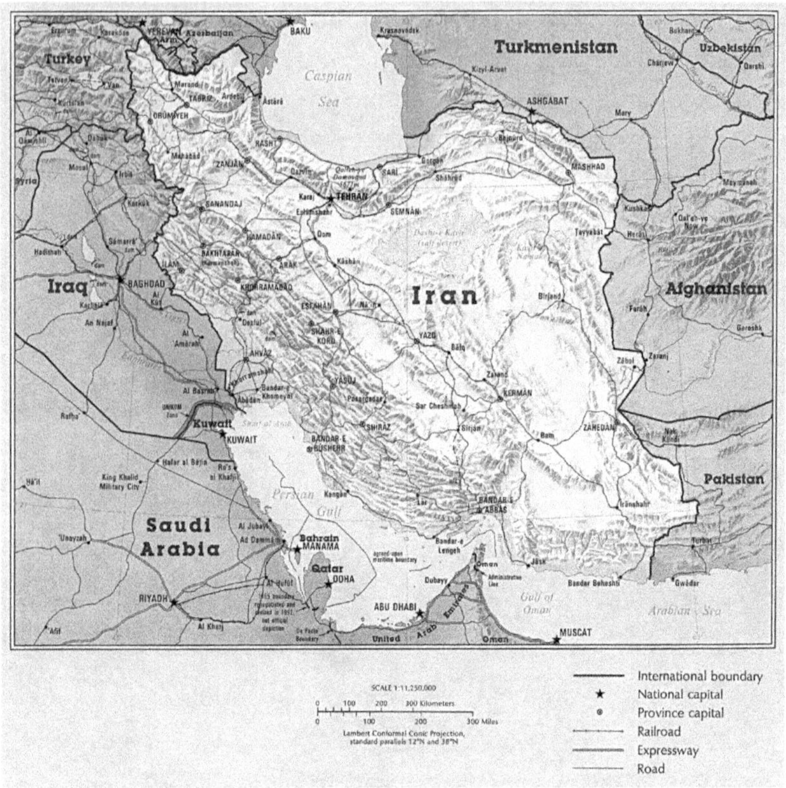

Now, look at the current map of Iran (Persia):

As you can see with traditional historical Christian presuppositions in place, there are reasons why Christian-American's have always supported Israelis' territorial and cultural integrity. It is because foundationally, there is an original boundary line for the first nation. The maps above are just a visual representation into why there is territorial and cultural disputes between modern-day Israel and the rest of the Middle East. Regardless of any new alliances between the Jewish and Muslim nations, Israel is lost in a sea of outright polarized middle eastern diplomacy. And according to Scripture (think Revelation and Isaiah) it's not getting any better.

The Jewish nation of Israel is the only one on earth who's blessed land was given to man directly by God Himself. Likewise, by way of Providence, North America was destined to bless and hold those Christian faithful in safety. The land was transformed, and over time the political landscape shifted into a Christian-American nation. Therefore this original Christian-American nation is the only one on earth who's blessed land was given to man through Divine Providence and the love of God Himself.

Throughout my scholarly studies, I've learned that God blesses those individuals who sacrifice their own gratifications and wants for the greater good of mankind. The Christ-centered missionaries who wandered the wildernesses of North America were prominent in sewing the fabric of North American history. They are long forgotten about but live on throughout literature. The American Founding Fathers were no different.

It is quite evident through their own achievements and undertakings in building America, that the distinct relationship between Israel and the United States of America plays into something unique. It is a bond so special that it lies in the heart of tradition. That is, a sacred bond bound to humanity both spiritually by God and by the laws of man. America and Israel will always, physically and in spirit, be united on earth.

WAS ROME REALLY ALL THAT GLORIOUS AND MIGHTY?

Was the Roman Empire really all that great and mighty? Sure it looked pretty and worked out well for some lengthy amount of time. But in the end, *who really* made out well? I know that the pro-life and pro-abortion movements are running at equal speed today, so how does this all-parallel Rome?

As I am writing out my manuscripts, I tend to run into many exciting events that occurred throughout history. I get this information from the root of its source. In doing so recently, I actually found some startling information on the Roman Empire towards its latter days. You see a lot of people these days comparing Rome to their own culture, especially its final collapse. Well if you want to get into parallels about morals and ethics, how about we try this one on for size from the *Preface (iv)* of *A Star in the West* by Elias Boudinot, L. L. D. (Trenton, NJ. 1816):

"Plutarch in his Morals, 1 vol. 96, says that [between 264-146 BC] the Lacedemonians [a regional Italian culture inside of the

Roman Empire] murdered their children who were deformed or had a bad constitution. The Romans were allowed by Romulus to destroy all their female children, except the eldest. Human sacrifices were offered up in almost all the eastern countries [of the Roman Empire]. Children were burnt alive by their own parents, and offered to Baal, Moloch, and other pretended deities."[35]

Mr. Hume says in his Essay on Political Science; the most illustrious period of the Roman history considered, in a political view, is that between the beginning of the first and the end of the last Punic war; yet at this very time, the horrid practice of poisoning was so common, that during part of a season, a praetor punished capitally, for this crime, above three thousand persons in 'a part of (enlightened) Italy and found information of this nature still multiplying."

Interesting parallels to a modern day and age...

35 Boudinot, Elias.*A Star in the West, Or, A Humble Attempt to Discover the Long Lost Ten Tribes of Israel, Preparatory to Their Return to Their Beloved City, Jerusalem.* 1816. https://www.canadiana.ca/view/oocihm.51551/13?r=0&s=1.

ORIGINS OF NATIVE NORTH AMERICA

The history of Indigenous contact *should be* taught differently in light of the absence of written documentation. It should be done with logic, reasoning, and science of course. The way American society has been taught the history of the world has been intentionally fractured since the start of the Industrial Revolution. Creation is what America was originally taught of human beginnings prior to this. Here, I still highlight the "pagan" acts and traditions of cannibalism as something that needs to be brought to light--given the lack of awareness to the very real cultural divide.

"It begins when the Flood subsides. Noah plants a vineyard, makes wine, and falls into a stupor in his tent. Ham . . . sees his father's nakedness and tells his two brothers what has happened.... When Noah wakes up and learns what has happened, he lays a curse not upon Ham but upon Ham's son: 'Accursed be Canaan. He shall be his brothers' meanest slave.' . . . Whizzing forward to the medieval versions we learn more about the nature of Ham's misdeeds. He mocked Noah's nakedness, and invited his brothers to do the same (which they refused). What is more, this is not the first of Ham's transgressions. When they had all been on the Ark together, Noah had insisted that everyone be sexually continent, but Ham, by the aid of a magic demon, slept with his wife..."[36] And the *Curse of Ham* was in effect.

The Tower of Babel in Mesopotamia was the next "Fall of Man." I wrote an article awhile back where I clarify the results of Babel and its destruction on humanity. The world was a wicked place in the days of Noah. Compared to most European lifestyles they were observed as disgraceful, disgusting, violent, immoral, and unethical societies and in those days, it was something horrific. Dr. David Leston wrote that "archaeologists have unearthed bodies of people who lived in Mesopotamia, they have found evidence that cannibalism was practiced. In short, this was a very brutal era, in which humanity showed little to no regard for one another."[37]

He goes on to mention that in "January 1996 National Geographic did a comparison between rodeo riders and their injuries, and skeletons uncovered from the time of Noah. They found striking similarities between the injuries of the two groups, suggesting that this was a very violent society. When people reject God and the boundaries and purposes that He has created for them, they become a law unto themselves, and society becomes weaker and more dangerous."[38] The net results are the same as always--extreme anarchy and a violent world. So, God flooded the world and spared the only honest and Godly man alive at the time. It was Noah who God gave the task of rebuilding civilization.

---

36 Braude, Benjamin. "The Sons of Noah and the Construction of Ethnic and Geographical Identities in the Medieval and Early Modern Periods." The William and Mary Quarterly 54, no. 1 (1997), 103. doi:10.2307/2953314.

37 Leston, Stephen, and Christopher D. Hudson. "From Creation to the Tower of Babel | The Age of Noah." In The Bible in World History: How History and Scripture Intersect, 31. Uhrichsville: Barbour Pub, 2011.

38 Leston.

It was right after the Flood that people would repopulate the Fertile Crescent (the middle east). This was a very fertile and agriculturally productive area which was quick to develop and fought over heavily. One of humankind's early technological developments was the ability to design, manipulate materials and make structures such as buildings. It was mankind's obligation from God to subdue the earth. He ultimately gave mankind all the faculties necessary to create great constructions. However, in man's rebellion against God, this gift was used in ways to honor men and not Him—such as The Tower of Babel. This attempt at building a ziggurat mega-structure was humankind's next attempt at playing God. Just a note here—it will blow your mind to look at the similarities in the Mesopotamian ziggurat of biblical days and a typical ziggurat from South America.

In Genesis 11, the tower planners said "Come, let us build ourselves a city and a tower with its top in the heavens, and let us make a name for ourselves, lest we be dispersed over the face of the whole earth." The planners of course were referring to making a name for mankind above God's name. God saw this ability of men to centralize power effectively for the purposes of glorifying themselves. He then—in an instant—created world languages to confuse the masses and dispersed them globally. This is where Dispersion across the globe took effect. This effectively explains human migration in the ice age, world language and similarities in technology worldwide.

The evidence offered by National Geographic parallels ancient cannibalism to what we see in Native North America (and globally). It makes sense that at dispersion why humankind had kept their basic tribal customs alive--without the cultural sustainability nor political liberty to sustain themselves after European contact. Cannibalism was a custom and ritual that was carried on and practiced by indigenous peoples since the beginnings... hence, the

"Curse of Ham."[39] Marshall Sahlins, an Anthropologist, viewed cannibalism as a variety of symbolism, cosmology, rituals, and traditions.[40] Sigmund Freud looked at cannibalism within the indigenous cultures as an underlying mental issue—psychoses.[41] Even serial killers have been known all throughout time have committed acts of cannibalism. I'm not saying this was the case, but it certainly represents something to take into consideration as a cultural practice.

The idea of the Portuguese in North Africa in the early 15th century having cannibalistic tendencies makes sense. Consider the technological example of human civilization and human capital, in whole, there was no advancement of "civilization" until after the printing press was invented by Gutenberg. Europe was still shut into Medieval living. It was still the Dark Ages, with pagan tendencies. I use the word "pagan" to describe non-Christian ritualistic practices.

It was mentioned that the "remnants of cannibalistic rituals could also be said to be found in explicit references, such as the [Catholic] Eucharist (in which worshipers consume ritual substitutes of the body and blood of Christ). Ironically, the early [Catholics] were called cannibals by the Romans because of the Eucharist."[42]

---

39 "DNA and Native Americans." Book of Mormon Evidence. Last modified October 16, 2019. https://bookofmormonevidence.org/dna-and-native-americans/.

40 Harris, Marvin. "'Cannibals and Kings': An Exchange." The New York Review of Books. Last modified November 21, 2015. https://www.nybooks.com/articles/1979/06/28/cannibals-and-kings-an-exchange/.

41 Freud, Sigmund. "Totem and Taboo; Resemblances Between the Psychic Lives of Savages and Neurotics." Internet Archive. Accessed December 14, 2020. https://archive.org/stream/totemtabooresemb00freu.

42 Allina, Eric. "The Zimba, the Portuguese, and Other Cannibals in Late Sixteenth-century Southeast Africa." Journal of Southern African

This explains the blending of Roman Catholic customs and traditions (which do not traditionally exist within Protestant Christian sects), as well as the mixing of tribal spirituality and customs in the Dark Ages. Thus, the Old-World Portuguese carried their blended Catholic and old ritualistic tribal customs into North Africa—engaging in their old pagan practices of feasting on human beings.

So, it happened also that the Taino conquest of the Siboney tribe (just before Columbus first landed) was executed in utter completion. Columbus wrote that he had met one Siboney survivor who communicated that the Taino were relentless, violent, taboo, and cannibalistic.[43] An invasion by the Taino, statistically, would have been the complete genocide of one culture. This annihilation of a people group matches or even exceeds the largest estimates of destruction by European diseases and exposure.[44]

It's a fair say that in the pre-Columbian world, wars, slavery, and complete annihilation may not have been uncommon after all. I mean, "one could legitimately argue that for many Amerindian people the expansion of the Huari, Aztec, and Inka empires was equally cataclysmic."[45] Especially in comparison to what followed after European contact. In this, the idea that Christopher and his European counterparts brought the idea of war and violence to a civilization (or world) that was previously untouched and unblemished is historically bankrupt.

Studies 37, no. 2 (2011), 211-227. doi:10.1080/03057070.2011.579433.

43 Morison, Samuel E. Admiral of the Ocean Sea: A Life of Christopher Columbus, 464. Morison Press, 2008.

44 Taylor, Alan. American Colonies, 38. London: Penguin, 2002. (Statistical Breakdown)

45 Santos-Granero, Fernando. Vital Enemies: Slavery, Predation, and the Amerindian Political Economy of Life, 6-7. Austin: University of Texas Press, 2010.

There has been scientific evidence, as suggested earlier, that makes cannibalism very widespread and indeed an ancient tribal global human practice. This would make sense considering the religious and sociopolitical foundations at that time.[46] It was part of the animistic tribal lifestyle that was inherited by the first generation of those original peoples dispersed at the Tower of Babel.[47]

46 Helmenstine, Ph.D, Anne M. "What You Need to Know About Bovine Spongiform Encephalopathy." ThoughtCo. Accessed December 14, 2020. https://www.thoughtco.com/mad-cow-disease-overview-602185.

47 Genesis 6:5 & 6:6, The Holy Bible.

SLAVERY: STILL OUR NATIONAL SIN

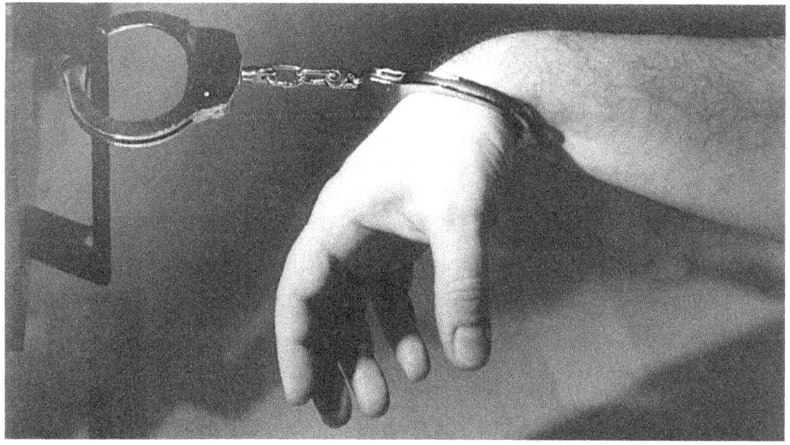

Congress in 1787 and 1789 would pass the Northwest Ordinance, which outlawed slavery in any newly created state of the Union. The federal government would also ban the exportation of slaves from any state within the Union in 1794. All intentions show of that generation that the eventual abolishment of slavery was their main intention.

God wanted to show the world how a Christian nation would attempt to deal with such a heavy-laden social problem. England outlawed slavery in 1834, and this was primarily due to the efforts of evangelical Christians. But the United States failed to address the issue of slavery just as God had intended. Slavery is a national sin, and one reason for this enabled failure is greed.

The famous inventor of the cotton gin Mr. Eli Whitney made his contraption well-renowned in 1783. This machine would end up making slavery much, much, much more profitable. The resulting effects of this new profit would rise a new generation of Americans with much less conviction on the matters of slavery than their fathers.

The rest of the nation, instead of dealing with the issue head-on, attempted to compromise. The trend of abolition came to a screeching halt in the South. And even churches began to (for the first-time ever) justify slavery by 1810. By then however, all slave trading had been banned, yet slave owning, became much more ingrained.[48]

The church body fractured over the idea of slavery, as when "in April 1808 when John Murphy, clerk of the church, rose from his seat and 'declared non-fellowship with the church on account of slavery.' Following Murphy's lead, Elijah Davidson then rose and withdrew from the church because it tolerated slaveholding among its members. In the following five months, two men and four women left the church for the same reasons.

Far from a singular event, this rupture was repeated in churches across the state and was the culmination to a decades-long debate within Baptist churches in the Upper South over the issue of slaveholding. Before the crisis was settled, Baptists would be forced to rethink their doctrines, worldview, and relationship to the new republic."

---

48 Dr. Beliles, Mark A., and Stephen K. Dr. McDowell. America's Providential History, 227. Charlottesville: Providence Foundation, 1989.

"As Baptists began to evangelize the Upper South, they addressed the complicated issue of slaves and slavery. Slaves were part of the early audiences for Baptist itinerants in the 1760s and 1770s, and, after the War for Independence, slaves began to join churches in increasing numbers. This phenomenon forced Baptists into the quagmire of slavery as they constructed a coherent theology and a network of churches in a revolutionary age.

The churches they built were biracial with white and black members. White and black evangelicals together faced the contradictions between their theology, which emphasized the equality of souls, and the institution of slavery, which reified inequality. Churches became the arenas in which southerners debated what slavery meant in an evangelical society and what religion meant in a slave society."[49]

It was the national sin of slavery that would cause the evangelical movement to seek to reform American society in the Civil War era and well into today.A combination of dumbed-down education, misinformation, and poor leadership has sunk our nation. Today's slave owners are not "the master," however, they surely have a say on "how, when, and why," and not until all of your debts are paid off. Today? Modern slavery is just a refined version of indentured servitude, that's coated with sugar.

49 Najar, Monica. 2005. ""Meddling with Emancipation": Baptists, Authority, and the Rift Over Slavery in the Upper South." Journal of the Early Republic 25 (2) (Summer): 157-186.

To Believe or Not? A Divided American Economy

To declare the many economic changes to early America as "truly revolutionary" would be to establish that America somehow "invented" success through capitalism. Many people today like to think of America as the foundational creator of evil corporate capitalism. That would in fact be misleading, as capitalism has been around since the medieval times. Historian Gilje and Fernand Braudel, both recognized and acknowledged from a communal standpoint that "the emergence of western capitalism to the development of city states at the end of the medieval period."[50]

America refined successful economics that brought her the success she earned. The issues lie within the secular paradigm that is overwhelmingly present in America. It seems that it was secularism that high-jacked America's traditional prosperity and

50 Gilje, Paul A. "The Rise of Capitalism in the Early Republic." *Journal of the Early Republic* 16, no. 2 (1996): 159-81. Accessed September 28, 2020. doi:10.2307/3124244.

punctually drove it off a cliff.[51]Secularism puts God completely out of the equation when it comes to ethics and morals.

Secularists hold the view that "religious considerations should be excluded from civil affairs or public education. Also, that "exclusive attention to the present life and its duties, and the relegation of all considerations regarding a future life to a secondary place; the system of the secularists; the ignoring or exclusion of religious duties, instruction, or considerations."[52]

An Honest Wealth of Nations

Historian Lamoreaux mentions, "Henretta has 'acknowledged the existence of capitalist values and activities among a portion of the rural population,' but he used the numerical subordination of that portion to justify his emphasis on 'a rather different worldview among the majority of farm families.' It is important to note, however, that many historians do not accept this characterization for farmers in the middle Atlantic and southern regions, whom they regard as much more oriented toward market production than farmers elsewhere."[53]

I find that the heart of economic success lies in a culture's religion. Thus, the primary reason that world nations are in poverty is due to a lack of spiritual resources and truth. When you compare the factors of production in Christian and secular societies, it clearly shows you why some countries are successful

51 *How to Understand the Purpose behind Humanism,* 7. Booklet published by Institute in Basic Youth Conflicts, 1983.

52 "Secularism." In *The American Heritage Dictionary of the English Language*, 5th ed. Boston: Houghton Mifflin, 2018.

53 Lamoreaux, Naomi R. 2003. "Rethinking the Transition to Capitalism in the Early American Northeast." *The Journal of American History* 90 (2) (09): 437-461.https://ezproxy.snhu.edu/login?qurl=https%3A%2F%2Fwww.proquest.com%2Fdocview%2F224892264%3Faccountid%3D3783.

and other fail. Historian Wolfe writes, "While men and women in every country try to multiply their human energies with the help of tools in order to transform natural resources into useful goods and services, Christian free societies generally do it more efficiently than others."[54]

A research study made by Dr. Browning of the different income ratios of differing nations and people groups reinforces this observation. He wrote that "between protestant and catholic groups it was noted consistently that the protestant countries had higher per capita income than the catholic countries. But those who were not Christian had no income or low incomes or were starving to death."[55]

Sure nations like Japan are successful, but the only reason they even made it there in the first place is because "they have simply imitated the principles and techniques on which America's original prosperity was built."[56]These are principles which actually grew out of our Christian-American society (and which have been seemingly abandoned today).

PROFIT MOTIVES

Man's material welfare increases in a Christian Society because Christian faith and character assist to "enlarge, vitalize, and improve" the key factors of economic production. Once again, Historian Wolfe writes, "The economic incentives of freedom are also important. To find and process natural resources such as oil and minerals is extremely costly. So is the protracted process of

54 Wolfe, CharlesH., and JamesB. Rose. "The Principle Approach to American Christian Economics." In *A Guide to American Christian Education for the Home and School, the Principle Approach*, 398. Palo Cedro, CA: American Christian History Institute, 1983.

55 Anthony, Greg. *Biblical Economics*, 13. 1988.

56 Wolfe, 398.

researching, developing, and producing new and more efficient power tools. The profit motive provides individuals with the needed incentive in a Christian free economy based on individual enterprise."

"History shows that in a Christian free economy... men tend to invent more and better tools, invest more in producing those tools, and use those tools more efficiently than in a secular society with limited economic freedom."[57]

If you look at the historical record of current events, there are many nations that have operated on a communistic style of economic principle. This kills off profit motive. As a reaction, these governments have slowly opened to allow more individual enterprise because it allows people to be more successful. China and Russia are two great examples here. Russia, in recent years, has begun to let "each farming family 2-3 acres of ground to operate privately and sell its produce in the local market. These tiny private farm plots produce more meat, vegetables and fruit than all of the huge government farms combined."[58]

So ultimately, communal farming with absolutely zero incentive and doesn't work for Christians who all have common visions, goals, and purposes. I mean look, the Pilgrims offered up a great example with the first couple years in America. They were bound to a communal contract with their financial backers over in England. It was the lack of incentive to work resulted in such poor crops, they almost starved off. Once Governor Bradford switched over to private enterprise, everyone was able to live abundantly off the land.[59]

57 Wolfe, 403.

58 Skousen, Leon. *Study Guide to the Making of America.*

59 Bradford, William. *Bradford's History "Of Plimoth Plantation": From the Original Manuscript; with a Report of the Proceedings Incident to the Return of the Manuscript to Massachusetts*, 162. 1898.

NEW MEXICO, 1581: AN ENCOUNTER OF GOD'S PROVIDENCE

Some call this a spectacular historical example of God's Providence. Others challenge it as pure luck. The North American Indian is vital in the grand design for the world's history. Their history plays an equally important role in the larger story in how history continues to be laid out for humanity. Their culture takes part in the same human history that God has had for all of humankind since the Creation and Adam and Eve.

Now, Providence is not just the name of a city in Rhode Island. Providence is a word that is generally defined as God's omnipresent and active role in the world's history. That means at any given time He may, or may not, intervene on humanity's behalf. Providence is also seen as historical proof through linking current events, the historical past, and Christianity.

Many people do not know that one of the first times mainland America was ever entered was by way of northern Mexico and the Spanish Europeans. It wasn't until 1598 that the Spanish would try to colonize New Mexico. An expedition of 400 soldiers headed north from Mexico City, led by devout Catholic explorer Don Juan de Oñate. This was the 2nd time that any European would touch mainland North America. It was also the 2nd time they would also have explicit experience with the Pueblo Indians, as one of the first few Indian tribes ever initially contacted.

The feelings and observations of divine authorship over the initial European discovery of New Mexico could not be truly understood without offering a final example of God's omnipresent works. Occurring shortly after this event, historian Villagra wrote of much hardship endured by Onate's expedition into indigenous and untraveled New Mexico.

"After many trials and many sufferings, [we] came in sight of a splendid pueblo. We gave it the name of' 'San Juan,' adding 'de los Caballeros' in memory of those noble sons who first raised in these barbarous regions the bloody tree upon which Christ perished for the redemption of mankind."[60]The task of desert exploration was no easy job. And the idea of "trials and many sufferings" shouldn't be taken out of context either. They were literally surviving.

60 Minge, WardA., Miguel Encinias, Alfred Rodriguez, JosephP. Sanchez, GasparP. De Villagra, and Larry Frank. "Historia de la Nueva Mexico, 1610: Gaspar Perez de Villagra." *The Western Historical Quarterly* 25, no. 2 (1994), 237. doi:10.2307/971486.

It was mentioned:"These men are forced at times to subsist on unsavory roots and unknown seeds, and even on the flesh of dogs, horses, and other animals whose flesh is most abhorrent to all civilized people. Through the snowy passes they blaze their way as a plow cuts a furrow through the soil. Often in the mountain fastnesses they escape in snowdrifts only by clinging to the tails of their horses…"

Upon making it to the Indian village,"The natives of this pueblo came forth and gladly shared their homes with us. Here the entire army made camp. One day, while the general was taking his meal, the savages began to raise such a frightful wail that we all thought the final day of judgment had arrived, when we would be called before the judgment seat of God to give our final accounting."

"Astonished and confused, we inquired the cause of such dreadful lamentations. The people answered that for a long time they had been praying to their gods for rain; that despite their prayers not a single cloud appeared to darken the heavens, and that unless the drought were broken all their hopes would be gone, for not a single plant would yield its crop."

"On hearing this, the commissary, and the good Fray [Father] Cristóbal, trusting in God from whom all our needs must come, commanded the Indians to cease their wailing, for they would offer prayers to God in heaven, asking Him to look down with pity, and, though they were disobedient children, to send abundant rains that the dying plants might revive and yield plentiful crops."

"The Indians were greatly pleased, and like little children who hush when they are given the things they have cried for, ceased their lamentations. Eagerly and anxiously they scanned the heavens, awaiting the promised rain. The next day at about the same hour in which they had set up their wail, the skies suddenly became dark, and the clouds of heaven opened and poured forth regular torrents of rain. The barbarians stood spellbound in awe and mute gratitude at the unbounding mercy of God…"[61]

God's omnipresence is literal. History is His story. Examples of Providence are well-documented all throughout history, including all American history. Humanity in all its ethnic make-up is part of His all perfectly written and final grand design.

61 Ward.

THE E.U.'S HADRON COLLIDER & THE TOWEL OF BABEL

Tower of Babel by Lucas van Valckenborch, 1594. In the Louvre Museum.

The original Hadron Collider in the E.U. wasn't enough, so they want to build it bigger.

Is this the modern parallel to the Tower of Babel from ancient Mesopotamia?

When we consider lessons being taught and learned throughout our lives, we don't necessarily think of these lessons starting at the very beginning of time. These lessons include the ethical and moral principles in which Christianity itself is based upon. Even further though, we never pull back far enough to see how lessons effect society and humankind as a whole unit. From the beginning mankind has chosen to take the path seemingly today more frequently traveled in poor decision making for achieving scientific greatness—all starting with Adam and Eve—with their choice to eat the apple from the forbidden Tree of Knowledge. Humanity didn't learn it's lesson from The Fall which shows us that humanity can't do it their own way. Adam and Eve were banished from the Garden of Eden. This ultimate expulsion sealed the fall of mankind.

The world was a wicked place in the days of Noah. Those disgraceful, disgusting, violent, immoral, and unethical societies in those days were something horrific. Dr. David Leston wrote that "archaeologists have unearthed bodies of people who lived in Mesopotamia, they have found evidence that cannibalism was practiced. In short, this was a very brutal era, in which humanity showed little to no regard for one another."[62]He goes on to mention that in "January 1996 National Geographic did a comparison between rodeo riders and their injuries, and skeletons uncovered from the time of Noah.

They found striking similarities between the injuries of the two groups, suggesting that this was a very violent society. When

62 Leston, Stephen, and ChristopherD. Hudson. "From Creation to the Tower of Babel | The Age of Noah." In *The Bible in World History: How History and Scripture Intersect*, 31. Uhrichsville: Barbour Pub, 2011.

people reject God and the boundaries and purposes that He has created for them, they become a law unto themselves, and society becomes weaker and more dangerous."[63]The net result? The same as always, extreme anarchy and a violent world. So, God flooded the world and spared the only honest and Godly man alive at the time. It was Noah who God gave the task of rebuilding civilization.

MAN'S REBELLION

It was right after the Flood that people would repopulate the Fertile Crescent (the middle east). This was a very fertile and agriculturally productive area which was quick to develop and fought over heavily. One of humankind's early technological developments was the ability to design, manipulate materials and make structures such as buildings. It was mankind's obligation from God to subdue the earth. He ultimately gave mankind all the faculties necessary to create great constructions. However, in man's rebellion against God, this gift was used in ways to honor men and not Him—such as The Tower of Babel. This attempt at building a ziggurat megastructure was humankinds next attempt at playing God. Just a note here—it will blow your mind to look at the similarities in the Mesopotamian ziggurat of biblical days and a typical ziggurat from South America.

In Genesis 11, the tower planners said "Come, let us build ourselves a city and a tower with its top in the heavens, and let us make a name for ourselves, lest we be dispersed over the face of the whole earth."[64]The planners of course were referring to making a name for mankind above God's name. God saw this ability of men to centralize power effectively for the purposes of glorifying themselves. He then—in an instant—created world languages to

63 Leston, 32.

64 The Holy Bible (NKJV) | Genesis 11:4.

confuse the masses and dispersed them globally. This effectively explains human migration in the ice age, world language and similarities in technology worldwide. Today, humankind over time has once again gathered to challenge God once again.

The Parallel

On January 15th, 2019—CERN unveiled plans for an even larger Large Hadron Collider, with a 100km (62-mile) circumference - about four times longer than the current machine. The Future Circular Collider (FCC) will be almost 10 times more powerful than the current machine too. CERN (European Organization for Nuclear Research) said the FCC, which should be in use by 2040, would "significantly expand our knowledge of matter and the universe".[65] It was built by theEuropean Organization for Nuclear Research(CERN) between 1998 and 2008 in collaboration with over 10,000 scientists and hundreds of universities and laboratories, as well as more than 100 countries.[66]The final end-game to this complex science experiment is the specific knowledge of this "God-particle" that adheres all of the atoms of physical matter together—which is where we get our physical reality from. This is arguably a tongue-in-cheek observation of humanities last parallel to the ancient Tower of Babel.

This time however, God is not going to come down to the Land of Shinar (the Fertile Crescent) to shake His head in humankinds disappointing direction. No. This should only serve humanity as a

---

65 "CERN Plans Even Larger Large Hadron Collider to Find More 'God Particles'." Worthy Christian News. Last modified January 16, 2019. https://www.worthynews.com/38497-cern-plans-even-larger-large-hadron-collider-to-find-more-god-particles.

66 "Large Hadron Collider." The Telegraph. Accessed December27,2019. https://www.telegraph.co.uk/science/large-hadron-collider/3351899/Large-Hadron-Collider-thirteen-ways-to-change-the-world.html.

reminder. A sign of the times that we live in today. In the Biblical sense, humanity did not learn it's lesson from The Fall. Nor did mankind learn it's lesson from The Flood. Nor did mankind learn from the freedom of slavery that Moses gave the Israelites from the Pharaoh in Egypt. Nor did mankind learn from Sodom and Gomorrah. Finally, mankind didn't learn either from the Tower of Babel. It is not unreasonable to suggest that Europe's Large Hadron Collider is civilizations last whole combined scientific effort to become God before humanity's final days.

RADICAL REPUBLICAN'S? THEY DO INDEED EXIST.

Not all Republicans agree with Republicans, and not all Democrats agree with Democrats. This is not just a fair estimation, but a genuine understanding that most of us can agree with.

Recently, a national news outlet released an article that mentioned that *The Lincoln Project* is working to de-rail the Christian political narrative. They represent a non-profit "political action committee that is composed of Republicans and ex-Republicans that seek to prevent Trump from winning re-election." They are running hard on all cylinders.

POLITICO maintains that both entities "officially formed a partnership on Wednesday as a means to capitalize on religious voters who dislike Trump or are unhappy with his handling of the COVID-19 pandemic as well as the black lives matter protests."[67]

"If there was ever a time when Republicans, especially people of faith can be moved, it's probably now," said Sarah Lenti, executive director at the Lincoln Project. "This is about doing the right thing for our country and that goes back to embracing Biblical principles, such as loving and caring for each other."

All throughout Trump's first term, many white evangelicals have expressed unwavering support for the President. But recently, many of Trump's more liberal Protestant and Catholic advocates are turning away from the president due to his handling of the COVID-19 pandemic.

"Vote for Common Good (VCG) and The Lincoln Project are seeking to push Joe Biden, a professing Roman Catholic, as a religious alternative for evangelical voters, many of whom are slated to vote for President Trump in the upcoming 2020 presidential election."[68]

---

67 'Never Trump' Republicans Team with Progressives to Convert the President's Religious Base." POLITICO. Last modified August 4, 2020.https://www.politico.com/news/2020/08/04/lincoln-project-gop-religious-base-joe-biden-391427.

68 'Never Trump' Republicans Team with Progressives to Convert the President's Religious Base." POLITICO. Last modified

The Radical Republicans were unmistakably for greater things within the Union. Just like their more moderate peers they wanted emancipation and removal of the racist KKK, however, it was the underhanded attack on Lincolns outlying principles that made this political group come to deliberately smear and attack the fair-minded Presidents good name.

At the end of 1863, Lincoln executed an order to "Reconstruct," or rebuild the South at the end of the Civil War. It was under the President's order that if 10% of the population in a state took an oath of loyalty to the federal government, the state would be allowed to declare a new state government recognized by the United States.

The Radical Republicans (congressmen) in office were angry by Lincoln's mild-mannered approach to what they viewed as almost treason—given his forgiving and light attitude towards the rebellious states that were (at the time) waging war against the Union. The Congressional bill was titled "Wade-Davis" which was named after two members of Congress.

Ultimately, this bill said that a majority of white citizens of a state that had openly rebelled against the federal government would be required to swear loyalty to the Union to be readmitted. Congress went on to approve the Wade-Davis Bill, and President Lincoln (in mid-1864) refused to sign the bill, thus letting the bill die at his desk.

The response to all of this was a group of Congressional Republicans responding by attacking Lincoln and his administration. The Radical Republicans even urged other Republicans to run against Lincoln in that same year's presidential election! By doing this, these Radical Congressmen became extremists

---

August 4, 2020.https://www.politico.com/news/2020/08/04/lincoln-project-gop-religious-base-joe-biden-391427.

to some degree and purposely alienated many other traditional Republicans.[69]

It is crucial, if not critical, to be very aware of those political and cultural interests in your own camp, as well as those in the opposition. Opportunity is ripe for those people with evil intentions looking to destroy your good works. However, this will only become a guarantee if you continue to remain politically and socially unaware.

69 Myers, Peter C. 2016. "Statesmanship and Reconstruction: Moderate versus Radical Republicans on Restoring the Union after the Civil War." *American Political Thought* 5 (1): 160–62.

CHRISTIANITY AND POLITICS ARE INSEPARABLE

There has been a lot of silence among the Christian population when it comes to the separation of the Bible and the political realm of society. There was a time in the not so far past that it was common for the typical American family to engage in worship, sermons, and politics—all under the church's roof and steeple, as well as inside the family home. It was only at the start of the 1960's that the American-Christian would start to feel an invisible suppression that would transcend on the free-right to discuss politics and religion at the dinner table.

The Christian Patriot was a sermon delivered at the South Congregational Church in Boston on July 5, 1840 By Rev. M. I. Motte. He started with Psalm 144:15– *Happy is that people, whose God is the Lord.* The preacher charismatically included

"Politics should be but one form of that charity which is the end of the divine law. One more of benevolence, one of the ministrations of philanthropy; and 'Holiness to the Lord' be inscribed over the portals of its halls of state and the chambers of its social festivals, as over the church door. Especially with us should this be aimed at on triple grounds. For, if political parties with us cannot be Christian parties, then are we a godless nation; there can be few Christians throughout the length and breadth of the land; since he, who is no politician under our institutions, is a solitary rarity."

"And how can we make a Christian nation? To become so, must be an individual, not a collective act. Legislation cannot do it if legislation would. Resolves of majorities, in caucus or in Congress, in towns or by states, or even unanimous votes, is not the way to affect it. The simple and sole process is for each person privately to resolve, for his single part, no influence in legislative deliberations, no political name or fame whatever, – nay, the shrinking woman and child, whose deliberations look not beyond the homestead, or who can legislate only over their own hearts, – these can add a stone, as truly as the mightiest statesman or the loudest demagogue, to build up the national temple to the Lord. Public opinion is the life-breath of our own government, and therefore to Christianize that, we have but to Christianize ourselves. O what it is ye may achieve! No such power as this is possessed by the subjects of any government but yours."[70]

---

70 Motte, M.I. "Sermon - Christian Patriot - Boston, 1840." WallBuilders. Last modified July 25, 2017.https://www.wallbuilders.com/

In this sermon, Rev. Motte made some great references to God-given liberty and where the government positions itself in relation to Christian-American citizens. No such power that we have as citizens to change the political spectrum than to vote and be active in politics and its related current events. The Founders would have completely agreed with this sermon in its entirety if it had not preceded the sermons date.

Dr. Stephen K. McDowell, President of Providence Foundation, mentions that the "Founders saw man from a Christian perspective; that is, man is sinful and in a fallen state. As such, they were careful to construct a form of government that would not entrust man with too much power, knowing that sinful man will tend to abuse power. John Adams wrote:

To expect self-denial from men, when they have a majority in their favor, and consequently power to gratify themselves, is to disbelieve all history and universal experience; it is to disbelieve Revelation and the Word of God, which informs us, the heart is deceitful above all things, and desperately wicked.... There is no man so blind as not to see, that to talk of founding a government upon a supposition that nations and great bodies of men, left to themselves, will practice a course of self-denial, is either to babble like a new-born infant, or to deceive like an unprincipled impostor."[71]

John Adams was referring to those elites and government forces that openly carried the majority power and influence in American politics. He references the fact that any expectations from those individuals who would rather gratify their own personal wants over the betterment of society as a whole nation would be downright absurd. Separating Christianity and politics

sermon-christian-patriot-boston-1840/.

71 Dr. McDowell, StephenK. "Christian Principles and Structure in the Constitution." Providence Foundation. Accessed July17,2020.https://www.providencefoundation.com/christian-principles-and-structure-in-the-constitution/.

just doesn't work. The Bible is entirely political in its entirety. It screams of pro-activity from the Christian population, especially in the participation of current-events and American politics:

"I don't talk politics and I don't talk religion! It's always guaranteed to start a fight." This quote is a commonly voiced occurrence that happens around the dinner table almost every single night. Or how about the younger generation? They are the ones that typically voice how uninterested in politics they are, or how it's "just not my thing." It is this combination of dismissive and overly passive remarks that sugar-coat what appears to be devotion. Any political engagement by the individual person in the church body is sometimes seen as making one somehow unfit for the gospel.

For all the rest of this people that have been flooded with TV ads, telemarketing campaigns, and the all-too-common negative vibes of politics—the above-mentioned quotes might be a tempting and attractive position to take. But for legitimate Creation-believing, and Bible-applying Christians, this is not a position that we can or even should accept.

The message that Dr. David Closson offers is that the "message of the gospel is that by grace through faith sinners can be reconciled with God (Ephesians 2:7-8). This message transforms individuals and enables them to lead godly lives. Mandated by Scripture (Matthew 28:19-20), Christians are charged to share the good news and disciple others in faith"

The Gospel is an all-inclusive message with critical implications for all-parts, and all-walks of life. This message should include of Christians actually engage the political process here in America. Active participation in the legal process that has been afforded to us all is the key here.

Dr. Closson, who serves as the Director of Christian Ethics and Biblical Worldview at Family Research Council wrote an article on four reasons Christians should truly care about politics beyond the home:

1. The Christian worldview speaks to all areas of life.

A frequently raised objection against Christian engagement with politics is that anything besides explicit preaching and teaching of the Bible is a distraction from the mission of the church. However, this is a limited understanding of the kingdom of God and contrary to examples in Scripture.

The Christian worldview provides a comprehensive understanding of reality. It speaks to all areas of life, including political engagement. In fact, the Bible speaks about civil government and provides examples of faithful engagement. In the Old Testament, Joseph and Daniel served in civil government, exerting influence to further the flourishing of their nations.

In the New Testament, Jesus engaged in holistic ministry, caring for the spiritual and physical needs of people. Feeding the hungry and healing diseases were an outworking and extension of the reconciliatory message of the gospel. Paul also advocates this approach: "As we have opportunity, let us do good to everyone" (Galatians 6:10). And: "For we are his workmanship, created in Christ Jesus for good works, which God prepared beforehand, that we should walk in them" (Ephesians 2:10).

Engaging in "good works" should include participating in the political process because of the legitimate and significant role of government. The decisions made by government have a substantial impact on people and the way we interact with them. A Christian worldview should include a political theology that recognizes every area of life must be included in the "good works" of believers, especially politics, an area with significant real-life implications for people.

2. Politics are unavoidable.

As "sojourners and exiles" (1 Peter 2:11), it can be tempting for Christians to adopt a mindset that earthly governing systems are inconsequential to the task of furthering the gospel. But ask a pastor in an underground church or a missionary attempting to access a closed country if politics are inconsequential. Religious liberty, passports and visas are not unnecessary luxuries but are often vital for pastors and missionaries seeking to preach and teach the gospel.

Augustine's City of God offers guidance on this point. Believers are citizens of the "City of God," but on this side of eternity, we also belong to the "City of Man" and therefore must be good citizens of both cities. There are biblical examples of how membership in the earthly city can be leveraged for furthering the reach of the heavenly. Paul's appeal to his Roman citizenship (Acts 16:37, 22:25) is a model of this.

In an American context, engaging these dual cities takes on added significance because of the words prefacing the Constitution: "We the people." In the United States, ultimate national sovereignty is entrusted to the people. James Madison explained that the "consent of the people" is the "pure original fountain of all legitimate authority." This reality makes politics unavoidable for American citizens who control their political future.

Because politics have real-world implications for Christian evangelism, missions and preaching the gospel, Christian's ought to engage the political process by leveraging their rightful authority, advocating for laws and policies that contribute to human flourishing.

3. We need to love our neighbor.

When questioned by religious authorities on the law, Jesus explained that loving God with heart, soul and mind was the greatest commandment (Matthew 22:37). He added that second in priority was: "You shall love your neighbor as yourself" (Matthew 22:39).

Followers of Christ are called to love and serve their neighbors (Matthew 28:19-20). When asked about the qualifications of "neighbor," Jesus told the parable of the Good Samaritan (Luke

10:25-37), indicating that irrespective of race, background, social status or occupation, neighborly love is owed.

In a very real sense, politics is one of the most important areas in which Christians demonstrate love to neighbor. In fact, how can Christians claim to care about others and not engage the arena that most profoundly shapes basic rights and freedoms? Caring for the hungry, thirsty, naked, sick, and lonely is important to Jesus and should be to His followers as well. Jesus said, "As you did it to one of the least of these you did it to me" (Matthew 25:40).

Fulfilling the biblical mandate to love neighbor and care for the "least of these" should be a priority for every believer. Again, a holistic approach is essential. Loving neighbor includes volunteering at a homeless shelter, as well as influencing laws that encourage human flourishing. Good government and laws are not negligible factors in the prosperity and freedom of a society.

For example, the majority of North Koreans are held in economic bondage by corrupt political forces, whereas in South Korea, citizens are given liberty and a system that encourages prosperity. The people of North Korea need more than food pantries and improved hospitals; they need political leadership and policies that recognize human rights. Advocating for these changes in totalitarian countries is crucial for loving our neighbors in oppressed areas.

Obedience to the golden rule includes seeking laws that protect unborn children, strengthen marriages and families, advocate for the vulnerable, and provide opportunity for flourishing. Politics is a means of effecting great change and must be engaged by Christians who love their neighbor.

4. Government restrains evil and promotes good.

Government derives its authority from God to promote good and restrain evil. This mandate is expressly stated in Romans 13:1-7. Elsewhere, Paul urges that prayers be made "for kings and all who are in high positions, that we may lead a peaceful and quiet life" (1 Timothy 2:1-2). Paul understood the need for Christian participation in government.

Government plays a role in the work of God's kingdom on earth. Good government encourages an environment conducive for people living peaceably, whereas bad government fosters unrest and instability. Because of sin, the legitimate institution of government has, at times, been used illegitimately throughout history. However, numerous examples persist of Christians reasserting their influence and redeeming government to promote good and restrain evil.

In How Christianity Changed the World, Alvin Schmidt documents Christian influence in government. Examples include outlawing infanticide, child abandonment and gladiatorial games in ancient Rome, ending the practice of human sacrifice among European cultures, banning pedophilia and polygamy, and prohibiting the burning of widows in India. William Wilberforce, a committed Christian, was the force behind the successful effort to abolish the slave trade in England. In the United States, two-thirds of abolitionists were Christian pastors. In the 1960's, Martin Luther King Jr., a Christian pastor, helped lead the civil rights movement against racial segregation and discrimination.

Carl Henry rightfully stated that Christians should "work through civil authority for the advancement of justice and human good" to provide "critical illumination, personal example, and vocational leadership." This has been the historic witness of Christians concerned about government promoting good and restraining evil.[72] Dr. Closson, great work! Point made.

72 Closson, David. "4 Reasons Christians Should Care About Politics." ERLC. Last modified August 4, 2015. https://erlc.com/resource-library/articles/4-reasons-christians-should-care-about-politics/.

Jeremiah 29:7 says: "But seek the welfare of the city where I have sent you into exile, and pray to the Lord on its behalf, for in its welfare you will find your welfare." Referring to Babylon, the prophet recognized that secular government served a legitimate purpose in God's plan for Israel. This is still true. Today, good governments promote literacy, advance just laws, provide religious liberty, and allow churches to preach and teach. Good government can serve as a conduit for the furthering of the gospel and human flourishing.

Christians in America, who live their lives in the public-venue, actually contribute spiritual values to the public. These carry moral and ethical weight when dealing with life's problems in public. When Christians pull back from politics, it opens up a degenerate vacuum that is open to outside influences. These negative influences actually pressure our government to work outside the framework chosen by God.

Essentially, politics effect government and absolutely effect its resulting legislation on the people. Politics shape society and influences how our nations culture changes and ultimately carries itself over time. It is because of what the Bible teaches and its inevitable effect on our American culture that Christians absolutely must care about current events, as well as politics.

THE TAKEOVER AND OCCUPATION OF B.I.A. HEADQUARTERS, 1972

The Bureau of Indian Affairs headquarters building was raided, ransacked, vandalized, and ultimately occupied for almost a week—November 3rd through the 9th of 1972...

Nearly 500 American Indians marching with the American Indian Movement (AIM – a liberally funded "progressive grass-roots" movement) ended their attention-grabbing parade called the Trail of Broken Treaties, in front of the BIA building in Washington D.C. This cross-country political parade was intended to highlight American Indian's social issues, such as their standard of living and obligated treaty rights as legally sovereign nations.

Activist and news contributor Bob Simpson would point out that "leaders of the Trail of Broken Treaties were negotiating with the Interior Department over the question of housing. Suddenly fighting broke out between several GSA security guards and a group of young Indians." He goes on to say that "apparently the guards misunderstood that the BIA had given the Indians permission to stay in the building past closing time. The guards were quickly overpowered and escorted from the building. Indians ran through the BIA building at 19th & Constitution breaking up furniture to barricade entrances and manufacture makeshift weapons. The occupation was on."[73]

73 Simpson, Robert. "Native Americans Take Over Bureau of Indian Affairs: 1972." Washington Area Spark. Last modified

Once inside the Indian Affair's building, protesters displayed their militant frustration towards the interior of the building.

May 10, 2013.https://washingtonareaspark.com/2013/03/26/native-americans-take-over-bureau-of-indian-affairs-1972/.

These radicals threw over furniture against windows and doors barricading against potential police interference. Other members of the group set multiple fires in different interior offices and vandalized the polished marble lobbies. Unfortunately, many historic documents were destroyed in the vandalism—with a second estimated valued loss of $700,000 to American taxpayers.[74]

The following day on November 4th—John Chancellor, reporting desk anchor for NBC News mentioned: "Several hundred American Indians remained in the Bureau of Indian Affairs building in Washington today. They took it over late yesterday after scuffles with police." Moments later, news field-anchor John Cochran reported live stating: "It was peaceful if not quiet at the Indian Affairs Bureau, but nothing was settled today. The Indians are waiting for The Administration to respond to their demands for reforms in the way the government deals with Indians. And they're asking for a decent place to eat and sleep while in Washington. Until they get it, they vow to stay in what they call 'their embassy.'"[75]

After a few days of altercation, the protesters began to run out of supplies. There was quickly little food and provision to sustain their opportunistic operation. The AIM protesters would not allow any police or government representatives to cross into the Bureau of Indian Affairs building. Because of this, two children of BIA employees were recruited (whether by coercion or

---

74 *The Washington Post* (Washington D.C.). «Amnesty Denied To Indians.» November 10, 1972.https://www.maquah.net/Historical/1972/images/72-11-10_amnesty_denied.jpg. *Note*: An initial first estimate was officialized at about $250,000 in damages within the building.

75 "Occupation of the Bureau of Indian Affairs" NBC News, New York, NY: NBC Universal, 11/03/1972. Accessed Sat Jan 11, 2020 from NBC Learn:https://highered.nbclearn.com/portal/site/HigherEd/browse/?cuecard=5170

force is unknown) to bring in supplies and rations for the volatile American Indian protesters.

It was reported that the radical AIM's actions created the loss, destruction, and theft of many historical records—mainly critical treaties, property deeds, and water rights documentation.[76]Even Indian officials stated that the consequences to the American Indian Movement's actions could set the North American Indian culture back 50 to 100 years—with a final estimated loss of nearly $2.28 million dollars in damages and theft by the hostile takeover of the BIA to the American taxpayer.[77]

In the end, it was the Nixon Administration who would secretly sign the "Menominee Restoration Act" on December 22nd, 1973. This policy would ultimately give the Menominee Indians full recognized tribal status by the U.S. government, and returning their land assets to trust status. Although it was only one tribe benefiting from this policy, it was a direct message sent to those who understood Nixon's political interests as a Democratic politician. Especially when it was obvious his administration passively gave in to the demands.

As I have researched, I have uncovered further evidence of the serious corruption and politicization that governmental and political entities tend to enable and create. We all know that the Nixon Administration was deemed corrupt, but just how deep did this administration sink in enabling the American Indian Movement's hostile takeover of the Bureau of Indian Affairs headquarters building? It's a great question. And the answer lies in the aforementioned involvement of certain political and governmental parties.

After the short BIA building takeover of 1971, there was research and formal organization prepared for and recruited by AIM. These consisted of sympathetic volunteer lawyers, professors, and scholars that would look up legislative policies, executive

---

76 *The Washington Post* (Washington D.C.). « Justice Eyes Way to Charge Indians." November 10, 1972.https://www.maquah.net/Historical/1972/images/72-11-1_justice_charge_indians.jpg.

77 *The Washington Post* (Washington D.C.). « Damage to BIA Third Heaviest Ever in U.S." November 11, 1972.https://www.maquah.net/Historical/1972/images/72-11-11_damage_to_BIA.jpg.

orders, as well as the BIA budget and its formal practices. The Nixon administration was said to have supported the AIM financially through proxy. That is, sympathetic groups were committed to the financial backing of AIM. Financial backing could only be committed through allotted special funds to meet the rapidly growing liberal civil rights movements of the 1970's.

The year prior to the BIA takeover in Washington D.C.—Democratic (and quite liberal) President Nixon stated in his 1970 address to Congress: "The special relationship between Indians and the Federal government is the result instead of solemn obligations which have been entered into by the United States Government. Down through the years, through written treaties and through formal and informal agreements, our government has made specific commitments to the Indian people.

For their part, the Indians have often surrendered claims to vast tracts of land and have accepted life on government reservations. In exchange, the government has agreed to provide community services such as health, education and public safety, services which would presumably allow Indian communities to enjoy a standard of living comparable to that of other Americans.

This goal, of course has never been achieved..."[78]

Younger American Indians and First Nations peoples would give the most support to the American Indian Movement's radical cause. The groups and entities found sympathetic to the BIA takeover of 1972 were:

- The National Indian Brotherhood of Canada
- Native American Civil Rights Fund
- Native Indian Youth Council
- National American Indian Council

78 Nixon, Richard. "Special Message to the Congress on Indian Affairs." The American Presidency Project. Last modified July 8, 1970.https://www.presidency.ucsb.edu/documents/special-message-the-congress-indian-affairs.

- National Council on Indian Work
- National Indian Leadership Training
- American Indian Committee on Alcohol and Drug Abuse

Other entities that endorsed and supported the radical takeover was:

- The Native American Women's Action Council
- United Native Americans
- National Indian Lutheran Board
- Coalition of Indian-Controlled School Boards
- Black Panther Party for Self Defense

There is almost always a political motive behind the current events that happen on the daily. Most of these above organizations are, or had been, funded by the Democratic Nixon Administration. Occupations, building takeovers, and progressive "grassroots movements" are all just a part of radical American history. It takes a certain rebellious ideology that is contrary to any kind of traditional American principle that enables this type of insubordinate behavior and defiant action.

This is also this same type of ideology and behavior that commits citizens to the destruction of their own history that we will never, ever see again in America. This past historical event should also concern every single one of us regarding corruption in politics, including political and cultural "grassroots" movements… because "movements" only carry temporary momentum, and are contrary to societal continuity and perseverance.

Isaiah 5:20 says, "*Woe to those who call evil good and good evil, who put darkness for light and light for darkness, who put bitter for sweet and sweet for bitter.*"

PROGRESSIVISM: DRYING THE AMERICAN SPIRIT

They say... that the Progressive Era brought in a liberal social movement to deal with the various social needs of that time. Policies in which would eventually turn into one big mass-social reform. Progressives supposedly turned their attention to problems such as class warfare, poverty, violence, racism, poor health. They seemed determined to eradicate through better education, a safer environment, an honest government, and an efficient workplace...

John Dewey, a pragmatic humanistic (opposite of Christianity) philosopher once said, "We want to bring all things educational together, to identify the lower and higher education, so that it shall be demonstrated to the eye that there is no lower or higher, but simply education."[79] Dewey should have ended it with "but simple education."

Dr. Stephen McDowell of Providence Foundation writes:

79 "Democracy and Education, by John Dewey." Accessed June5,2020. https://www.gutenberg.org/files/852/852-h/852-h.htm.

"According to the National Commission on Excellence in Education, America is 'A Nation at Risk.' The 1980's report stated: 'If an unfriendly foreign power had attempted to impose on America the mediocre educational performance that exists today, we might well have viewed it as an act of war.' The consequences of this poor performance are not only declining knowledge but also declining morality, both of which are necessary for a free and prosperous nation. The mediocrity is primarily due to a state monopolized educational system that has rejected its Christian foundation, replacing it with a secular ideology that teaches man is the ultimate authority and source of truth."[80]

"Contrary to the belief of many 'educrats,' the underlying problem is not financial but ideological. We have replaced a Christian philosophy with a secular philosophy of education. The Apostle Paul warns us: "See to it that no one takes you captive through philosophy and empty deception, according to the tradition of men, according to the elementary principles of the world, rather than according to Christ" (Col. 2:8)."[81]

And if that doesn't explain it clearly, try this on for size:

"Comparing the Christian and humanistic philosophies of law reveals why the left has such apoplectic rage at having lost power and why they are willing to do anything to regain it, while conservatives accept liberals ruling with relative calm."

"Law, from a Christian perspective and as the Founders of America viewed it, originates in the will of God, revealed in general to man through nature and his conscience, and more specifically in the revelation of the Scriptures. Law from a humanistic view is rooted in man, ultimately autonomous man, but practically in the state, and in the consensus of the majority, or of a powerful minority."

"From a Biblical perspective man is fallen and fallible, has a sinful nature, and thus needs to be restrained. The Biblical purpose of civil law is to restrain the evil action of men in society. True law reveals what is right and wrong, and hence, exposes lawbreakers. But law in itself cannot produce what is right, nor can it change the heart or attitude of man; therefore, the Christian acknowledges the inability to legislate "good," or to make people moral

80 McDowell, StephenK. "A Nation at Risk: Changing Textbooks Reveal the Secularization of American Education." Providence Foundation. Last modified June 19, 2018.https://providencefoundation.com/a-nation-at-risk-changing-textbooks-reveal-the-secularization-of-american-education/.

81 McDowell.

by-passing laws. However, the Christian recognizes the moral basis of all laws. All laws everywhere are based upon the moral presuppositions of the lawmakers. Laws against murder reflect a moral belief. Laws against theft are based upon the command to not steal. All law has a moral concern. The important question to the Christian is 'whose morality does it legislate?'"

"Humanists see the evils in society and in man but explain them differently than Christians. To the humanist there is no higher being than man. There is no incarnate Savior. From a humanistic perspective there is no hope of internal regeneration to save man, therefore, any salvation or transformation that occurs in men or nations must come from man. Historically, humanistic man has tended to use the instrument of law and government to attempt to bring such a transformation or 'salvation.'"

"Having no other means of provision, of salvation, or of peace, humanistic man attempts to regulate and provide all things through government and law. It is only through the force of law that evil will be eliminated, and utopia established on earth. Humanistic law is used to promote and advance humanistic morals. Such law, in conjunction with a corresponding educational system, is the only hope humanistic man has of establishing a 'saved' or 'righteous' — that is, good and progressing — society."

"To restate this, if there is no God who redeems man internally, then any elimination of problems brought on by what is in the heart of man must be done by man — often collective man and his government. The attempt will thus be made by government (at least those that have a vision for a progressing society) to use the instrument of law to bring more peace and goodwill among men and to eliminate all that is negative, such as poverty, crime, war, disease, prejudice, and ignorance."

"People with this worldview will also often look to government to provide their own personal material needs, and they usually vote for those who promise them the most. Therefore, it is not surprising that in the last election (as well as all recent elections) the vast majority of people receiving food stamps, public housing, Medicaid, disability, Obamacare subsidies, and various welfare benefits voted for liberal Democrats, who promised to continue and/or expand such programs."[82]

There are quite reasonable, and logical explanations for why certain individuals, societal entities, and leftist government have turned America into the breeding ground for vice, hostility, and confusion that we see around us every single day we step outside of our homes. This is not a fiction dystopian; this is a non-fiction reality that needs to be addressed with righteous continuity and perseverance. I fear that without pro-activity on our part; one day soon all of the practical ways to make money, how you teach your children, how you treat your health, and how you divvy up your own personal time will be completely framed-up by government and government proxies with no room for you to move socially, economically, or politically.

Sadly, a larger and larger percentage of the American population is knowingly and unknowingly inviting a personal life under a communal and socialist ideology. In a country where the government provides the mass majority of societies safety net—you really do start to see the demoralizing fruits of this condescending phenomena over a couple of decades. The intimate sense of self-value and worth that this nation is founded and built upon, are the same virtuous principles which have traditionally produced the truth in America's success over societal progresses and advancements.

Our liberty is like a thick onion that is being peeled in layers; the more we see liberal government intrusively providing for the

82 McDowell, StephenK. "Why Do the Leftists Rage? A War of Worldviews." Providence Foundation. Last Modified February 15, 2017. https://providencefoundation.com/why-do-the-leftists-rage-a-war-of-worldviews/.

private citizenry of America—the less liberty we will have to enjoy. We are, and we will run out of the "freedom-of-option" that us American's have come to appreciate. Get involved with your church, community and in local politics. It's not an obligation, it's truly an American responsibility. And, as always, continue to seek the truth…

A Truth Behind God and the Confederacy

The legacy of the Civil War is profound. Ramifications are felt all the way into our more modern times and today it's in the fabric of our culture. It certainly was not a matter of "hero" and "villain"—because we all know that in life there is good and evil. It could be said that for some, the envisioning of good and evil is a regional concept. That is, as long as good and evil exist, it will fit into whatever struggle meets an individual or groups own societal political narrative.

While I myself would never condone the Confederacy, it is in our more recent history that American symbols for southern tradition and culture were either destroyed or removed. Whatever the matter, destroying history is a sin. At least in these eyes. General Robert E. Lee actually has a biography that is incredible. I highly recommend reading it if you ever have the time. Lee was a man of prestige, honor, and righteousness—even before and after the American Civil War.

A great example to give is this: In a conversation with a minister one Sunday morning shortly after the start of the war. Lee was asked: "Is it your expectation that the issue of this war will be to perpetuate the institution of slavery?" Lee replied: "The future is in the hands of Providence, but if the slaves of the South were mine, I would surrender them all without a struggle to avert a war."[83] This is just one fraction of the truthful character General Lee showed not just in public, but during private conversation. And besides virtues, his military record was pretty spectacular regardless of his personal decision and belief to take on the calling as a revered Confederate general.

I think we all have a pretty good idea that the Union was blessed by God throughout the Civil War. God is good, and a *confederacy* against God (and His ultimate final planning) is evil. Did you know that the Bible speaks of the Confederacy and Confederates throughout the Scriptures? True stuff. The Bible gives the origin and meaning behind "Confederate" and "Confederacy." Check this out: Isaiah 7:2, and 8:12—speaks of a confederate rebellion . Also, even Genesis 14:13 speaks of those being confederate with Abram. Not convinced yet? Check out Obadiah 7 and Psalm 83:5 too!

---

83 Beliles, Mark A., and Stephen K. McDowell. "The War for the Union." In *America's Providential History*, 3rd ed., 233. Charlottesville, 2010. Print.

The Confederacy was not just the title of a grey-dawning, slave-owning, southern aristocracy—it is a deep-seated principle cloaked in rebellion. Ultimately, there was no way God was going to sanction the South to be allowed to continue slavery in a truly free society… especially after God Himself sent Moses to free the Israelites from captivity in Egypt. Answers-in-Genesis, ran by Ken Ham, also the Founder of the Creation Museum, explains that "[From Noah] Ham's son Mizraim founded Egypt (still called Mizraim in Hebrew). Egypt was the first recorded nation in the Bible to have harsh slavery and it was imposed on Joseph, the son of Israel, in 1728 BC, according to Archbishop Ussher. Later, the Egyptians were slave masters to the rest of the Israelites, and Moses, by the hand of God, freed them."[84]

Under this same principle, is it not unreasonable to believe that Abraham Lincoln was brought up to his position to ultimately lead the southern slaves to freedom? Is it not unreasonable to believe that God sanctioned the Union's cause? If America was founded by Divine Providence, that is, through the guidance and intervention of God in its national inception; the last bastion of liberty and freedom on the planet—than just howunreasonable is it to believe that the *Confederacy* was not included within God's final plan?

And look, even further, Romans 8:31 states "*If God is for us, Who can be against us?*" It's simple. Providentially, if the Union were sanctioned by God to achieve victory and emancipation, there was absolutely no way outside of a daydream that the South would have won the Civil War in the first place.

---

84 Hodge, Bodie, and PaulK. Taylor. "The Bible and Slavery." Answers in Genesis. Last modified February 2, 2007. https://answersingenesis.org/bible-history/the-bible-and-slavery/.

"And we know that all things work together for good to those who love God, to thosewho are the called according toHispurpose." – Romans 8:28

THE U.S. COAST GUARD IN WORLD WAR TWO: MISSION EFFECTIVE

The U.S. Coast Guard Escanaba crew waiting to board a lifeboat in World War Two.

The U.S. Coast Guard played a key role during World War Two. Here, I clarify the varied and important role the service played in saving lives and contributing to the US and Allied Powers' war efforts around the globe:

The naval history of World War II is propense, given the size of the war and participation of nations involved. And more often than not, the United States Navy offers a huge and understandingly repetitive presence over the naval history of WWII. More often than not however, it is the United States Coast Guard's selfless service and true expense that is lost in that large shadow.

In November of 1941, the Coast Guard went from the Treasury Department to the Department of the Navy; so perhaps this was why the histories of WWII usually look past or only shortly mention the Coast Guard's priceless role in the great event. The United States declared war after the Japanese surprise bombing of Pearl Harbor and spent four years and eight months in the fray of internal and external conflict. It was this catalyst that the Coast

Guard's accountabilities to its service to country extended significantly, being valued more than just search-and-rescue, and law enforcement; now it was seen completely integrating militarily.[85]

The Coast Guard was actually involved in some very significant events in World War II. How effective were they? Seaman John Cullen, for instance, was walking the beach performing routine night patrol on the 13th of June of 1942. During his walk Seaman Cullen observed four Germans landing ashore, on a saboteur mission code-named *Operation Pastorius.* Seaman Cullen of the U.S. Coast Guard was *actually* the *first* American who came into contact with the enemy on the shores of mainland USA during WWII.[86] Another incident, CGC Icarus (WPC-110), a 165-ft patrol boat that once had been a rumrunner chaser during Prohibition, put a German U-352 under water on 9 May 1942, off the south coast of Charleston, South Carolina.[87] The Icarus crew took on 33 prisoners that day. They were the first German nationals taken in combat as prisoners by any U.S. armed force.[88]

During the entire length of WWII, U.S. Coast Guard elements sent 12 German and two Japanese submarines to the bottom of the ocean and would end up capturing two German warships. Finally,Signalman 1stClass Douglas A. Munrowas the only Coast Guardsman to be awarded the Medal of Honor. It was at the 2ndBattle of the Matanikau, Petty Officer Munro was tasked with leading the extraction of 400 United States Marines that had been beaten and overrun on the Japanese island. Munro used a 7.62 mm deck-mounted machine gun aboard his "Higgins

---

85 Bishop, Eleanor C. 1989.*Prints in the sand: the U.S. Coast Guard Beach Patrol in World War II.* Missoula, Mont: Pictorial Histories Pub. Co.https://archive.org/details/printsinsand00bish_0.

86 Walling, Michael G. 2008. "Dangerous Duty in the North Atlantic." *Naval History.*

87 Walling, 204-207.

88 Walling, 208.

Boat" to direct a suppressing fire against the Japanese positions as the other recovery boats took on the beaten and battered American Marines. He would end up selflessly putting himself between heavy fire from the Japanese forces and the U.S. Marines – leading the ten-landing craft and saving all five-hundred U.S. Marines, including 25 wounded, all escaped.[89]

A DRIVING FORCE

The United States Coast Guard *was* and continues to remain to be the most professional, elite, and underappreciated service out of the 5 branches of the U.S. Armed Forces. In WWII history,

89 Quesada, Alejandro de. 2011. *US Coast Guard in World War II.* Oxford: Osprey Publishing Ltd.WorldCat Reference Center, Online. p. 97.

evidence suggests the U.S. Coast Guard was more involved than the history books lead on. So, just *how effective* was the U.S. Coast Guard during World War II? Admiral Chester Nimitz highly praised the valuable and selfless performance of Coast Guard men and women in World War II by stating: "I know of no instance wherein they did not acquit themselves in the highest traditions of their Service, or prove themselves worthy of their Service motto, 'Semper Paratus'—'Always Ready.'"[90]

It was back in 1837 that the Coast Guard went even further with the order to save lives and property. The main functions of the service were no longer just law enforcement related, but now relied upon as the saviors of life and property with maritime safety taking up an equally important role. For a branch of service that has *less people* serving in it than the New York City Police Department, it always seems it is the U.S. Coast Guard that always stands out at the end of their long days. The Coast Guard has been involved in *every single one of our nation's wars at sea* – along the side of their Navy counterparts. These brief aforementioned illustrations stand as evidence to the examples of the Coast Guard, its crew, and its mission capabilities. Of course, all of this centered around being a 5thmilitary branch of service, with all privileges entitled.

There is *another* historical event that would equal *silence* to the incredible effectiveness of the Coast Guard's mission capabilities. Signalman 1st Class Douglas A. Munro is the aforementioned Coast Guardsman who would equally compare in this *quiet and unpromoted* glory in while their service. It's interesting in part to think about just *how* unrecognized the service is. Proof? Half of my recruit training company didn't even know the Coast Guard

90 U.S. Coast Guard, Statistical Division/Historical Section, Public Information Division, *The Coast Guard At War* (Washington: Public Information Division, U.S. Coast Guard Headquarters, 30 June 1944–1 January 1954), (monograph 7).

was a seagoing service when asked about it by the Company Commanders.[91] If recruits are naïve about the mission, is it unreasonable to assume that the general public wouldn't have an idea of Coast Guard's mission effectiveness? Of course not.

The mission effectiveness pre-dating our modern era is apparent when looking back in the historical entries. The Revenue Cutter Service (as it used to be known) was re-named United States Coast Guard in 1915, after the U.S. Government observed just *how* effective they were as a wartime *and* non-wartime entity.[92] It is amazing that with such successes in the field and low publicity, both publicly and within the other four military branches, the Coast Guard still continues to remain *the most* underappreciated branch of the services.

UNDERAPPRECIATE AND EFFECTIVE

Overall, the Coast Guard performed valiantly with statistics of their own military accomplishments during WWII. 12 submarines were sunk in the Atlantic Theater by Coast Guard Cutters, Coast Guard Anti-Sub Planes, and Coast Guard-crewed naval vessels. The U.S. Coast Guard documented that from 1941, to the end of the war, Coast Guard crews had served successfully on-board Navy attack transports (APs & APAs) and with personnel to spare. They continue on to say, "It was an obvious choice to let the Coast Guard continue to assist in manning various ships of the ever-increasing Navy fleet. They readily took to all of the various

91 "USCG Basic Training Experience, Delta-162" Daniel L. Smith, 2002.

92 U.S. Coast Guard, Statistical Division/Historical Section, Public Information Division, *The Coast Guard At War* (Washington: Public Information Division, U.S. Coast Guard Headquarters, 30 June 1944–1 January 1954), (Monograph 17)

types of landing craft utilized by the Navy, including the Landing Craft Infantry, Large, or LCI(L)s, beginning in 1943."[93]

Technologically, the Coast Guard headed a cooperative effort between scientists and the U.S. Navy, to develop the Long-Range Navigation (LORAN) system. The Coast Guard stated that, "Pulse transmission of radio waves permits LORAN to measure the time a signal travels. This allows an infinite number of lines of position to be placed over the Earth's surface by radio. Using special charts and a simple receiver, a plane or ship could determine its general location within a few miles by longitude and latitude. LORAN is the first use of electronic navigation, precursor to Global Positioning System (GPS)."[94] In June of 1942, legislation in the Executive Branch changed the face of the U.S. Coast Guard forever sealing their fate as a military service. Further, the presidential decree allowed for the centralization of the Coast Guard as the premier multi-mission branch of service.

According to the U.S. Coast Guard Historians Office:

"The President delegates port-security to the Coast Guard. Responsibilities included: Control of anchorage and movement of all vessels in port; Issuance of identification cards and the supervision of access to vessels and waterfront facilities; Fire-prevention measures including inspections, recommendations and enforcement; Firefighting activities, including use of fire-boats,

93 "U.S. Coast Guard Manned LCI(L)'s." U.S. Department of Defense. Accessed April1,2019. https://media.defense.gov/2017/Aug/08/2001789793/-1/-1/0/LCIS.PDF.

94 "Timeline 1900's - 2000's." United States Coast Guard (USCG) Historian's Office. Accessed April19,2019. https://www.history.uscg.mil/Complete-Time-Line/Time-Line-1900-2000/.

trailer pumps and other extinguishing agents; Supervision of the loading and stowage of explosives and military ammunition; Boarding and examination of vessels in port; Sealing of vessels' radios; Licensing of vessels for movement in local waters and for departure; Guarding of important facilities; Enforcement of all regulations governing vessels and waterfront security; Maintenance of water patrols; General enforcement of federal laws on navigable waters and other miscellaneous duties."[95]

Handling and piloting these small boats in the rough surf is most certainly a specialized skill. Additionally, this type of emphasized skillset was not common among men in the Navy. Not guys in the Coast Guard though. Many of the coxswains (small boat handlers) had learned this skill from pushing boats through the surf at coastal lifesaving stations. Coast Guard small boat handlers were actually only at lifesaving stations. Most were highly seasoned small-boat handlers, as this proved valuable to the service. Maneuvering landing craft through strong currents, reefs, sand bars and heavy surf, is what these lifesavers excel at. Further, their aid to amphibious operations during the entirety of the war is infinite.

RISING UP

The experience of these surf-men was priceless during amphibious operations. The Coast Guard's surf-men acted as trainers and coaches to the U.S. Navy small boatmen trying to learn the complexities of controlling craft in the rough waters and heavy seas. During the early period of WWII, thousands of Coast Guard and Navy personnel were skilled and apt to handle landing craft in preparation for the beaches.

Part of that landing craft mission was landing troops at D-Day, but given the sheer size of the operation, the Navy and

95 Historian's Office.

Army asked that the Coast Guard also provide a flotilla of ships to rescue Americans stranded in the water. The Coastie's punctually rose-up to complete the challenge, pulling from their daily experience in saving lives for over a century. The Coast Guards Cutters and other small-craft went to war on D-Day. They were literally behind the first wave of landing craft hitting the beaches of Normandy. They had been told to stay two miles away from the shoreline, but most of the Coastie's took their craft closer to shore where they could rescue more lives.

The United States Coast Guard pulled over 400 men out of the water that day. One small boat named "Homing Pigeon," manned by the Coast Guard, rescued 126 lives in one day.[96] It was the Coast Guard Cutters *Eastwind* and *Southwind* that would end upcapturing the Nazi vessel *Externsteine* off the coast of Greenland doing weather and supply duty after a brief firefight with nobody killed. The Coast Guardsmen gave the newly captured Nazi ship the name USS *Eastbreeze* and placed 37 men on board to man the vessel. *Eastbreeze* would end up sailing to Boston where the U.S. Navy renamed her USS *Callao*. Nazi supply vessel *Externsteine* was the only enemy ship captured while at sea by any U.S. naval forces during World War II.

What was the scope of the Coast Guard's rescue operations in WWII? A thorough examination of the United States military's records in the European phase of the war will reveal just how operationally effective the small services were outside of battle. 4,243 servicemen and merchant mariners were saved, and of these 1,658 survivors were picked up from being torpedoed along the Atlantic, Gulf of Mexico and the Caribbean. 810 souls were saved in the North Atlantic, and in the Mediterranean 115 saved.

---

96 Christy, Gabe. "How 60 Coast Guard Cutters Saved Over 400 Men On D-Day." WAR HISTORY ONLINE. Last modified September 14, 2017. https://www.warhistoryonline.com/world-war-ii/60-coast-guard-cutters-saved-400-men-d-day.html.

Further, 1,660 were saved from rescue cutters from the English Channel at D-Day. The fact is almost four and a half million fighting soldiers would embark by ship, to fight the enemy in Europe and Africa. Of all who were deployed, 3,954 were lost at sea.

THE TOUGH KEEP GOING

Over the course of World War Two, the U.S. Coast Guard remained completely active with the remaining landing forces until Japan surrendered. Other operations that contributed to the Coastie's efforts were mine-sweeping off the coasts during occupation. At the finish of major military operations in the Pacific, the soldiers., sailors, and airmen being ferried home by the Coast Guard would come to know the last ride home as… "Magic Carpet" rides. These rides home would have to have been one of the most relieving moments of any war wearied serviceman.

The Coast Guard contributed as much as any other branch of service to the war effort as part of the amphibious forces in the Pacific theatre of war. The men of this nation's smallest branch of service, – smaller than the N.Y.P.D. to be exact – proved as heroic and valiant as the men in the other branches. The Secretary of the Navy James Forrestal, in 1946, would stand on the podium and publicly state that during the war the United States Coast Guard "earned the highest respect and deepest appreciation of the Navy and Marine Corps. Its performance of duty has been without exception in keeping with the highest traditions of service." [97]

The fact of the matter is… *"Their experience in operating in all types of surf conditions as well as on the high seas made the Coast*

97 "What's in the Coast Guard's Secret Sauce for High Retention?" Federal News Network. Last modified January 16, 2018. https://federalnewsnetwork.com/dod-personnel-notebook/2018/01/whats-in-the-coast-guards-secret-sauce-for-high-retention/.

Guard crews a valuable addition to the Allied invasion fleets."[98] The United States Coast Guard continues to be the most elite branch of service operational today, also making the Coast Guard statistically, the best the five branches of military have to offer. The truth is that for being the most underappreciated branch of service; the men and women of the Coast Guard display their *moral* and *ethical* principles in the line of duty.[99] They truly were *mission effective* in WWII.

---

98 "What's in the Coast Guard's Secret Sauce for High Retention?" Federal News Network. Last modified January 16, 2018. https://federalnewsnetwork.com/dod-personnel-notebook/2018/01/whats-in-the-coast-guards-secret-sauce-for-high-retention/.

99 "From the Homefront: Top 10 Things We Wish People Knew About Coast Guard Life « Coast Guard All Hands." Coast Guard All Hands. Last modified February 5, 2014. https://allhands.coastguard.dodlive.mil/2014/02/05/from-the-homefront-top-10-things-we-wish-people-knew-about-coast-guard-life/.

THE AMERICAN CIVIL WAR: AN ONGOING 'SHADOW WAR '

It's far from over. In fact, it was never over. Here's a historical clarification to give an insight and some background information into the political 'shadow-war' occurring today in Washington DC and within states nationwide. And that is just the fallout of the ongoing American Civil War. American Historian's James McPherson & James Hogue, both prominent intellectuals whose area of expertise are in the Era of the Civil War and Reconstruction, gave an eye-opening account on the forecast of the Democratic Party's intentions for America in 1857 and beyond:

"*Slavery lies at the root of all shame, poverty, ignorance, tyranny, and imbecility...*"With a direct emphasis on the rogue political tactics used to obligate the whole mass of society,"*the lords of the lash*"(speaking of Democratic politicians and business elites) who"*are not only absolute masters of blacks [but] of all non-slaveholding whites, whose freedom is merely nominal, and whose unparalleled literacy and degradation is purposely and fiendishly perpetuated.*"[100]

R. H. Purdom would give a common man's warningearly:"*Decided course for the speedy suppression of the intolerable abuses*"taken on by white workers was absolutely necessary for the "*permanent welfare of the institution of slavery itself.*"[2] Mr. Purdom was a master mechanic who stood up to address a meeting in Jackson, Mississippi. He gave a stark warning to the elite's controlling the southern economy. By this point, even the poor working white class were ready to turn coat on their own institutions—and their own people.

In September of 1865, a prominent leading Democratic politician (just recently pardoned by the federal government after losing the Civil War) publicly scoffed at any idea of the Democratic party remaining loyal or remaining to have any type of good behavior towards the newly re-establish United States government. Even Wade Hampton, one of the South's wealthiest elite farmers (and a rebel hero) would mention immediately after the Civil War that it "*isour duty*" (talking of the post-war Confederates who were legally pardoned of treason) to support the President of the United States, however their loyalty to the new government would only

100 McPherson, James M., and James K. Hogue. "The Problems of Peace and Presidential Reconstruction, 1865." In *Ordeal by Fire: The Civil War and Reconstruction*, 543. New York: McGraw-Hill, 2009.

stay intact if "*he manifests a disposition to restore all our rights as a sovereign State.*"[101]

Even though rebellious military action ceased to be weeks after the loss, the Democratic party of the post-Civil War period only declared a momentary political ceasefire. And although formally, they did not willingly capitulate to the federal government (the Union) at the moment of military surrender. During this moment between April 9th and November 6th in 1865, a nearly invisible shadow war marked the 'beginning of the end' for the future of political and social cohesion within the United States of America.

Democrats had regained power in most Southern states by the late 1870s. Later, this period came to be referred to as "Redemption". From 1890–1908, the Democrats passed statutes and amendments to their state constitutions that effectively disenfranchised most African Americans and tens of thousands of poor whites. They did this through devices such as poll taxes to vote and literacy tests to "qualify" (among other underhanded tactics). By the late 1950s, the Democratic Party again began to embrace the Civil Rights Movement, and the old argument that Southern whites had to vote for Democrats "to protect racial segregation" grew weaker.

The Democratic party realized that regardless the outcomes of the Civil War and Reconstruction, the policy of "slavery-by-color" was over. Even segregation became an option not viable to their party's ethics, which is to oppress the poor regardless of color. So how did they do this? Modernization had brought factories, national businesses, and a more diverse culture to cities such as Atlanta, Dallas, Charlotte, and Houston. This attracted millions of northern migrants, including many African Americans. They gave

101 Beatty, Jack. "The Problems of Peace and Presidential Reconstruction, 1865." In *Age of Betrayal: The Triumph of Money in America, 1865-1900*, 543. New York: Vintage, 2008.

priority to modernization and economic growth over preservation of the "old ways" of the Democratic party. With the Southern economy being agricultural, and more recently industrial -- the Southern economy (owned by the majority Democratic elites) shifted their thought process towards mass-manipulation.

In other words,over the years, they knowingly shifted their political and social policy of human slavery inward -- meaning slavery is now not just for people of color or of poverty, but all those people in our communities nationwide that are easily manipulated, fooled, or inherently ignorant.

Between 1865 and the late-1880's, prices were falling, and people's incomes were increasing six-fold--offering American's more purchasing power.[102] The politicians of the New South began feeling the pressures of big businesses complaints that the increased wages were rising faster than factories and companies could produce. It is because of this major economic shift that the attack on the greedy worker was to begin. There was another shift as well. A social one. Now that the freedmen (former slaves) and previously non-slaveholding whites, were able to climb the free-market ladder unhindered. For the Democratic party, it was time to shift the focus to social and economic slavery--because slavery by color would be considered racist by today's standards--something that Democrats apparently insist they are not.

"*Cut their wages to begin with. Make them work harder. To align their interests with their employers, put wage earners on piecework* (part-time). *Above everything, do something to stop skilled workers from setting the pace of production and spreading to co-workers their spirit of 'manly' resistance to speed-ups"* (hostile resistance to forced increase in manual labor). Much like the post-Modern Institutions of Fast Food, Gas, and Retail, one laborer wrote: "*You start in to*

102 "Mechanical Association," Mississippian State Gazette, Dec. 29, 1858, 3.

be a man, but you become more and more a machine.... It's like any severe labor. It drags you down mentally and morally, just as it does physically."[103] Of course the Iron Workers during those times had it painstakingly hard physically, but the shift today has moved to being considerably exhaustive mentally, especially in our more recent times here in the United States.

The point made here is that historically speaking, the Democratic party has a proven track record of corruption, a complete absence of ethic, and a total incompatibility to the foundational principles behind the United States Constitution, the Bill of Rights, and the Declaration of Independence. Modern attempts at enabling 'neo-slavery' are the pacification of the general public (desensitization through all entertainment) and general misinformation of current and past-events; led by the 'Democrat-friendly' liberal media moguls in Hollywierd.

Today, Republicans are screaming at American's to "*get out and live!*" They want to encourage financial independence and societal success. The Democrats are screaming at American's to "*stay home and save lives!*" At this point, for what? One Democratic politician was quoted recently as telling American's that they should just stay home and "get paid" with the federalgovernment paying out a basic universal income for everybody. And in the future? Who knows, but the way things look, it could possibly by something as simple as misleading everybody into eventually doing everything from home anyways--and only home.[104]

103 Perrow, Charles. "A Society of Organizations." Theory and Society 20 (1991), 791. doi:10.1007/bf00678095.

104 Chris Talgo, Opinion Contributor. "Universal Basic Income and the End of the Republic." TheHill. Last modified May 12, 2020. https://thehill.com/opinion/finance/497244-universal-basic-income-and-the-end-of-the-republic.`

It is apparent through history's documentation that 'Neo-Slavery' is the Democratic party's modern endgame. At least it seems that way. Enough said.

The Democratic Establishment: A Series of Corruption and Lies

When the 1st President of the United States was leaving his prestigious office, he projected onto the people one of the most insightful speeches in American history. In 1796 George Washington would observe major trends in factionalism occurring under the noses of American's politically, and in his same speech, would also give one of the starkest warnings to all those paying attention:

"...Men may endeavor to excite a belief, that there is a real difference of local interests and views. One of the expedients of party [in order] to acquire influence within particular districts is to misrepresent the opinions and aims of other districts,...The alternate dominion of one faction over another, sharpened by the spirit of revenge...will gradually incline the minds of men to seek security and repose in the absolute power of an individual;... (also) it opens the door to foreign influence and corruption, which find a facilitated access to the government itself through the channels of party passions."[105]

Further he wrote, "you should properly estimate the immense value of your national Union to your collective and individual happiness; indignantly frowning upon the first dawning of every attempt to alienate any portion of our country from the rest. ... Your Union ought to be considered as a main prop of your liberty, and the love of one ought to endear to you the preservation of the other."[106]

Ultimately, Washington was giving a dark forecast of what he saw becoming of the new American government. Originally a government mostly joined in unity, quickly became saturated with social undercurrents, that started to drag down any cohesion in American culture and politics. It began with differing ideals that started with the emergence of the early American colonies,

105 Beliles, MarkA., and StephenK. McDowell. "The War for the Union." In *America's Providential History*, 3rded., 225-26. Charlottesville: Providence Foundation, 2010. (See also: Washington's Farewell Address, 1796)

106 Beliles & McDowell.

which were an import from Great Britain. An agrarian lifestyle with their own differing denominations of Christianity fomented the ideals and daily life that governed their people. With the very rapid expansion in farming and textiles, came political influences (lobbying) that became a crucial part of keeping slavery alive in the more Southern states.

With the educational growth of Social Darwinism (that is, human evolution and a meaningless yet very materialistic life--thanks to Karl Marx in 1844), came the idea that God was an outdated crutch; used by an outdated faith, by ideologically outdated people, who lack the means for social and political success. The quick separation of 'God and State' began to take hold towards the latter half of the 19th century. It is this interpretation of evolutionary tendencies, creating a "vogue of social Darwinism" which "discouraged governmental intervention [on] behalf of Negroes as well as underprivileged groups"—including "poor white people."[107]"It encouraged the belief that a solution to the race problem could only evolve slowly as the Negroes gradually improved themselves."[108]

SATURATED IN CORRUPTION

The two-decades that precluded the Civil War proved a "critical juncture" for the United States as a joined Union. Historian Kenneth Stampp holds firm that starting in the early 1800s –… sociologists, anthropologists, and psychologists (mostly secular) presented what they regarded as convincing evidence of innate racial traits-evidence indicating that Negroes were intellectually

107 Smith, Daniel L. "The Atlantic Slave Trade & Poor White People." complexamerica.org. Last modified February 17, 2020.https://www.complexamerica.org/blog/the-atlantic-slave-trade-poor-white-people.

108 Stampp, Kenneth M. "I: The Tragic Legend of Reconstruction." In *The Era of Reconstruction, 1865-1877*, 20-22. New York: Vintage, 1965.

inferior to whites and had distinctive emotional characteristics. It was the social scientists that supplied the racists of the late nineteenth and early-twentieth centuries with something that antebellum pro-slavery writer had always lacked: a respectable scientific argument."[109]

In the 1870s, the South's "natural leaders" officially took back office from designated regional Southern leaders and restore civil control of the Southern states from the Union military's governmental authority. Starting almost immediately after the Civil War, the legally pardoned (for varying levels of treason) bureaucrats of the Democratic party would be busted for embezzling over $1,378,000 between the 1860s and the 1880s. According to the Bureau of Labor Statistics, that would be about"$27,151,333.59in 2020."[110]One editor of a Southern newspaper would write that an "infamous ring" of "corrupt office seekers… [had] debauched the ballot boxes, raised taxes, and plunged States into debt."[111]

Another Democratic politician was quoted as stating: "Sir, it is no secret that there has not been a full vote and a fair count… since 1875" Further he says, "In other words we have been stuffing ballot boxes, committing perjury, and here and there in the state carrying the elections by fraud and violence…No man can be in favor of perpetuating the election methods which have prevailed… since 1875 who is not a moral idiot."[112]Corruption was not just directly in politics either. Corruption has got to be sustainable for the needs to meet the ends. And, if you are corrupt, you would put together a plan to push a false narrative. The same politi-

109 Stampp.

110 "$1,378,000 in 1870 ⊠ 2020 | Inflation Calculator." U.S. Inflation Calculator: 1635⊠2020, Department of Labor Data. Accessed May7,2020.https://www.in2013dollars.com/us/inflation/1870?amount=1378000.

111 Stampp, "The Tragic Legend of Reconstruction," 178-79.

112 Stampp, 178-179.

cians would indoctrinate future generations, by manipulating the American educational system—economically and financially.

Secular elites in public schools and prominent universities across the country (lobbied by certain government officials) would aggressively push and expand on Godless education, and on gaining a solid foothold on the public education system. This should clearly explain the push into secular reasoning; that is, the absence of God and His influence in American politics and culture. This is critical to understand that the entire design of the post-Civil War Democratic party was realigned ideologically to continue an ongoing subvert war on the federal government… a shadow-war for political power.

LEVERAGING INDIRECT POLITICAL POWER

After the Civil War, "Harvard was taken over by Unitarians, and as the quality of public education declined, Horace Mann convinced Massachusetts that the answer was to let civil government take charge of it instead of the private sector."[113] Ultimately this was the 'beginning of the end' to wipe away Christianity from American government—eroding the morals and ethics from the famous "Protestant Ethic." To break the will of a people—to enable social and economic slavery on a post-Civil War American society—would be to begin at the source of where all decision making begins.

What one learns through life's professional dealings, formal education, and personal experiences will always shape one's mind and one's thoughts. It's important to note that regardless of current political arguments, there is always a truth behind what motivates people—and politicians. The fact of the matter is this: The Democratic Party, historically, has always largely been a

113 Beliles & McDowell. "The American Apostasy & Decline," 253.

political party of deception, aristocracy, and fundamental slavery. It is the way of the world, and unless things change significantly (which will never happen)… it shall always remain.

America's Social Malfunction:A Brief History

Little Circus to the Big Show

P.T. Barnum is a man who unquestionably changed the world of entertainment within America's culture. He used a principle business technique of "rational recreation" that would end up becoming a national "norm" for American families everywhere. He would take the thematic archaisms of dramatic plays and mix them with the upstanding ideals of individual and family. This type of script writing would allow for his succession of new brand of entertainment. One great example is Barnum's dime museum which featured tightrope artists and "educational" depictions of biblical events surrounding them.

The 1860's to the 1890's was the beginnings of a new modern-day enlightenment, comparable to that of the Enlightenment of the 17th and 18th centuries. In that time however, their movement was one of intellectual ideas in Europe. They would use reason to pull themselves from the dark ages, question traditional authority and embrace the possibility that humankind could be improved through logical and rational change. The difference between then and our contemporary renaissance that we have experienced in our times is one that has embraced technology (like phones and television) in the place of logic and reason.[114]

Broadcasted and televised mass media arrived on the scene in the 1890's. The first entertainment pushed to the public was boxing matches set in storefronts or a burlesque scene in one of many penny arcade peep show boxes. These along with candy machines, coin-operated phonographs, and fortune telling games. The ultimate push by media moguls here was to give the busy working man quick doses of instant gratification. It worked. In 1905 the media giants would bring nickelodeon (short films) to the big screen. These 10-minute segments would feature slapstick comedy and adventure. By 1910—full blown movie theatres (upscale) were offering classy amenities compared to that of the penny arcades.

Films would offer the American public visual stories of alluring love interests, criminal success, and power. This would further give the public an intimate view of fantastic story's told that resonated with the people in general. The result of this thought process is this: "I can live my life like that." This pipeline of entertainment would end up fast tracking consequences for American society. Although filled with a "cross-cultural" appeal to all social classes in America, this form of entertainment would begin to loosen the fabric that would keep the country woven together. This new cultural acceptance of appearance, dress, music halls, and amusement parks became a mass commodity for everybody. And also a newly accepted necessity.[115]

Eating It All Up

114 "Enlightenment." Encyclopedia Britannica. Accessed October17,2019.

115 "Enlightenment." Encyclopedia Britannica. Accessed October17,2019. http://www.britannica.com/event/Enlightenment-European-history.

Fun, fashion, and fantasy goods would come out of the marketing and advertising piped through these entertainment fast-tracks. A release from traditional boredom and a new form of youthful energy. A gathering of individuality, liberty, self-expression would begin to subside during this period as the American public was underhandedly being silenced, separated, and increasingly brought-together by the "dream factories" in Hollywood and New York City. The mass change in public thinking related to this phenomena was more surprising to those in media and government than they expected. Fast forward fifty-years and the mass emergence of consumerism would show its face and TV would become a family member.

It is really important to mention this fact before continuing forward: By 1957, the average viewer was viewing 420 advertisements in one week. A lot! Considering the old hand-made function of advertising. One station would show 50-ads in two-hours on one station in 1964. The TV-set would become a nearly perfect expression of American suburban family life. TV would come to project domestic family-lives inside of the home (according to Hollywierd) and also warn people of urban-dangers in action-adventure shows. All of this to culminate in enticing viewers through ads to shopping malls and fast-food joints. Ultimately, it would go to reinforce a new trend (established by the radio) of "living room privacy" and a new national entertainment culture.

American materialistic behaviors really started emerging forefront by the 1930's, where the need for instant self-gratification and a certain emphasized want for individual attentions. For example, drive in's, quick-serve diners, dance clubs, social clubs, pool-halls, the list could drive on! These venues all served as a catalyst for American materialism which *foundationally* expressed the *new* cultural ideas of America. These are certainly liberal ideas of a self-interest approach in a speedy lifestyle. This also resulted in enabling emphasis on certain unethical and immoral counter-principles, which has saturated our service-based culture of liberty and democracy.

With little consequences from these self-destructive and humiliating behaviors; the result of this consumerist lifestyle is an American society filled with narcissistic, self-centered, attention hungry people—still all looking for more. They aptly look to make ends meet for financial gain in whatever way possible, all while continually propping up their unattainable dreams. The issue of societal division is of course in reference to the materialistic behaviors of Americans.

Instant gratification has caused the need for instant attention… and public *"likes."* It seems that a majority of Americans these days *living life by* way of social media and television could definitely have the potential to be *far more* personable, thoughtful, skillful, creative, and generally well-rounded than they are nowadays.[116]America has lost her majority wealth in human capital (people who have invested in themselves by formal education and work experience) to blatant irrational behavior, which as a result have become completely detrimental to society.

IN THE END IT'S BLURRED LINES

The typical American consumer is most impacted by the issues of social division. More importantly, targeted audiences are more susceptible to the further divisions that consumerism tends to fuel in people. American families nationwide are vulnerable to the social separation that consumer behaviors have result from. Further, negative moral and ethical marketing targeting men, women, and children alike have aggravated the issue.

116 Ritzer, George. "The Irrationality of Rationality." In *The McDonaldization of Society*, pp. 16. Thousand Oaks, CA: SAGE Publications, 2018.

Consumer behaviors as a result, have stoked individual forms of division through one's own psyche, such as not living to moral and ethical personal standards set down by America's founders. Often times it seems more and more often that individuals leave behind their family morals and values when out in the public scene. I mean, who hasn't heard about a Wal-Mart fight on Black Friday?

It is important for the typical American to understand that *consumer behaviors* are not normal. In fact, Forbes is actually promoting the soul-killing marketing strategy of instant-gratification to other corporations world-wide.[117]Is this not an attack on the family at home? It's been blatant for quite some time. It is important to clarify that these associated consumerist behaviors create *no tolerance for delay* in public (even private) venues.[118]

Richard Sweeney, a University Librarian, wrote a report on consumerist behaviors in Millennial's and the social impatience further proving social division (and frustration): "Millennial's, by their own admission, have no tolerance for delays. They expect their services instantly when they are ready. They require almost constant feedback to know how they are progressing. Their worst nightmare is when they are delayed, required to wait in line, or have to deal with some other unproductive process. Their desire for speed and efficiency cannot be overestimated. The need for speedy satisfaction, or as some believe instant gratification, permeates virtually all of their service expectations."[119]

---

117 Wertz, Jia. "Why Instant Gratification Is The One Marketing Tactic Companies Should Focus On Right Now." Forbes. Last modified May 1, 2018. https://www.forbes.com/sites/jiawertz/2018/04/30/why-instant-gratification-is-the-one-marketing-tactic-companies-should-focus-on-right-now/.

118 Sweeney, Richard. "Millennial Behaviors & Demographics." *University Librarian, New Jersey Institute of Technology*, December 2006, 10.

119 Sweeney.

The speed today that one takes in information is unprecedented with its resulting effect of consumer behaviors on the American public. Instant gratification is the result of globalizations far reaching effects on personal convenience. Receiving material and/or information at extremely fast speeds only exacerbates the personal issues for any American family; with an immediate effect on social impatience and a seemingly endless need for the self-gratification that instant information provides. It is with this blazingly fast speed at which information travels, that we as people keep our senses submerged in entertainment and distractions.

We need to understand how today's marketing and entertainment effectively *dis-enables* individuals by constraining them intellectually, motivationally, and ethically. People tend to cut corners a lot more, to make their ends justify their means. This is an affecting consumer behavior, and as a result contributes to negative social divide. We live in a systematized world and have been since the inception of McDonald›s. This chain of systematization has further cut back on the need for human capital (educated people). The end result is the *dumbing down* (for lack of better words) of American society.

Researchers at the University of California, San Francisco have discovered that the controlled information from syndicated network television stations, have led to an arbitrary intelligence decrease in individuals that spend two to three hours a day soaked in media.[120]In terms of social media, it has desensitized individuals to what would be considered a "typical" social life. Impatience, self-gratification, and a desire for more pleasure – is by far the most typical of resulting consumer behaviors. I suggest collecting, reorganizing, and reinforcing upright moral and ethical

120 "Watching Lots of TV 'makes You Stupid?" The Independent. Last modified December 3, 2015. https://www.independent.co.uk/news/science/watching-lots-of-tv-makes-you-stupid-says-american-universities-a6759026.html.

values through daily contact with family members, friends, and stranger. It most certainly is one of the first steps towards positive navigation through our American mess that we call society.

2 Timothy 3:1-5 says, "But know this, that in the last days perilous times will come: For men will be lovers of themselves, lovers of money, boasters, proud, blasphemers, disobedient to parents, unthankful, unholy, unloving, unforgiving, slanderers, without self-control, brutal, despisers of good, traitors, headstrong, haughty, lovers of pleasure rather than lovers of God, having a form of godliness but denying its power. And from such people turn away!"

Proverbs 14:34 says, "Righteousness exalts a nation, But sin is a reproach to any people."

A War Economy, Rationing, and "Victory Gardens"

Service on the Home Front by Louis Hirshman and William Tasker.

A *World War* economy is taking obvious shape in a virus ridden and conflict inflamed world. In complete global unison, all nations from around the globe have entered into a literal wartime economy.

There is nothing figurative about that. A wartime socioeconomic life includes strict rationing, curfews, forced closures of social events and public venues. These are serious limitations on typical freedoms most Americans take for granted, such as the ability to hang out at the park on a Saturday to BBQ with friends and family, or the impulse ability to buy as much food and gas as you want too whenever you want too.

Curfews are imposed on the public to keep casualties minimal in wartime. Propaganda and rhetoric are important to pay attention too as well by leading officials. These are typically national promotional narratives that are composed by government and media agencies. These are entities who work in concert to promote a visual and audial sense of national unity in times of war or unrest.

In WWII you would have seen a "WORK OR FIGHT" propaganda campaign pushed nationally."Rosie the Riveter"posters beckoned housewives to leave the home and enter the nation's factories. According to the *Independence Hall Association*, "About 6.5 million females entered the workforce during the war years, many for the first time. African Americans continued the Great Migration northward, filling vacated factory jobs. Mexican Americans were courted to cross the border to assist with the harvest season in the *BRACERO* GUEST-WORKER PROGRAM. Thousands of retirees went back on the job, and more and more teenagers pitched in to fill the demand for new labor."[121]

In WWI, the United States was able to raise up enough food and raw materials by voluntary measures only. With the outbreak of WWII and the growing size of the population, federal officials concluded that rationing was the best and only option for demands to be met. Books of stamps were sent out to every

121 Independence Hall Association. "The American Homefront." US History. Accessed March22,2020.https://www.ushistory.org/us/51b.asp.

American family. These stamps allowed you to purchase gasoline, sugar, meat, butter, canned foods, fuel oil, shoes, and rubber. Any purchase of these supplies without a wartime issued stamp was made illegal.

In fact, the Office of Censorship decreed a code of conduct for newspapers, magazines, and broadcasters. The OOC did not use government censors to pre-approve all articles and radio programs, however. The government relied on voluntary cooperation to avoid sensitive topics. Military movements, weather predictions, and the locations of high-ranking officials would have been information considered beneficial to the enemy. Journalists however were not required to publish positive propaganda only like in WWII.[122]

The office did not use government censors to pre-approve all articles and radio programs. It relied on voluntary cooperation to avoid subjects, such as troop movements, weather forecasts, and the travels of the President, that might aid the enemy. Journalists did not have to publish positive propaganda, unlike during World War I. The Office of War Information would sponsor posters and public rallies to appeal to patriotic Americans. Entertainers like Bing Crosby; also including filmmakers like Frank Capra, would all help to boost continuity in public morale.

Energy supply was a sacrifice on its own to American's equally. To conserve the national gasoline and oil supply for war, "Victory Speed Limits" were imposed.[123] This required Americans to drive at a slower speed. Rotating blackouts were instituted to conserve petroleum, which was to be shipped overseas for the war effort.

---

122 "Secrets of Victory: The Office of Censorship and The American Press and Radio in World War II." Central Intelligence Agency. Last modified 0715.https://www.cia.gov/library/center-for-the-study-of-intelligence/csi-publications/csi-studies/studies/vol46no3/article10.html.

123 Perrone, Catherine. "Home Front Friday: The "Victory Speed" Limit." The National WWII Museum Blog. Last modified January 11, 2017. https://www.nww2m.com/2015/12/home-front-friday-get-in-the-scrap/.

On the Home-front, social groups such as the Boy Scouts and Salvation Army would lead scrap metal and donation drives. You would have seen large consumer products like refrigerators and vehicles just not being made at all. Backyard gardens would end up bringing in 8-million tons of food for Americans all over the country.[124]

The successes made on public advancement by the effects of the World Wars were one's demonstrative of American unity. This is an American unity that is continually solidified in history. Out of these great World Wars would bring in new economic industries like Synthetics, and old industries would be brought back to life. All of this action was made on behalf of tremendous costs to the typical American citizen and taxpayer.

Of course today is a much different situation as we are all being led to believe that this is a unified global World War on a biological virus. You can kill off influenza as quickly as you can stop global acts of terrorism. Much like the revolving door of response and retaliation, it tends to be cyclical. You cannot declare war on a virus. That is not viable to any society. So how should it be dealt with? Well that's not my job to figure out. However the way I see it today and moving forward, you simply can't expect American society to ever be the same again. The politicization of today's ugly biological event signals a shift in how American and global society operates from here on out. Like all World Wars, even when the enemy is a biological one, it is politicized to some degree.

124 Future Farmers of America. "Victory Gardens History." Accessed March22,2020.https://www.futurefarmers.com/victorygardens/history.html.

THE 1918 INFLUENZA AND COVID-19: A WAKE-UP CALL

So here we are. In a great modern-day national and statewide quarantined lock-down. A new procedure for every American today. Has anyone ever heard of the Great Flu of 1918? The Great Influenza of 1918 might arguably resemble the CoVID-19 flu that we are seeing today, at least to some degree. For instance, we notice that Iran is dealing with the brunt of the viral outbreak with over 1,000 casualties that they are allowing to be officially reported inside of their borders.[125] Of course they are also hyping up the situation by calling for "over one-million deaths" from this unfriendly influenza.[126] During the Great Influenza the global economic and social effects were catastrophic for everybody at that time, not just Asia and the Middle East.

---

125 "Iran Coronavirus Death Toll Passes 600, Syria Shuts Schools." Worthy Christian News. Last modified March 14, 2020.https://www.worthynews.com/47764-iran-coronavirus-death-toll-passes-600-syria-shuts-schools.

126 "Coronavirus Ravages Middle East As Iran Warns of 'Millions' of Deaths." Worthy Christian News. Last modified March 17, 2020. https://www.worthynews.com/47862-coronavirus-ravages-middle-east-as-iran-warns-of-millions-of-deaths.

The U.S. Center for Disease Control and Prevention wrote: "The 1918 influenza pandemic was the most severe pandemic in recent history. It was caused by an H1N1 virus with genes of avian origin. Although there is not universal consensus regarding where the virus originated (although China rumored to be the likely cause), it spread worldwide during 1918-1919. In the United States, it was first identified in military personnel in spring 1918.

"It is estimated that about 500 million people or one-third of the world's population became infected with this virus. The number of deaths was estimated to be at least 50 million worldwide with about 675,000 occurring in the United States. Mortality was high in people younger than 5 years old, 20-40 years old, and 65 years and older. The high mortality in healthy people, including those in the 20 to 40-year age group, was a unique feature of this pandemic.

"While the 1918 H1N1 virus has been synthesized and evaluated, the properties that made it so devastating are not well understood. With no vaccine to protect against influenza infection and no antibiotics to treat secondary bacterial infections that can be associated with influenza infections, control efforts worldwide were limited to non-pharmaceutical interventions such as isolation, quarantine, good personal hygiene, use of disinfectants, and limitations of public gatherings, which were applied unevenly."[127]

After doing some research, I found out that Iran (Persia) suffered the most casualties from the Great Influenza of 1918. A telegram from The Minister in Persia (Caldwell) to the Secretary of State. "American Relief Commission *en route* to Persia (Iran), headed by DoctorJudson, are scattered on the Pacific at Seattle, Bombay, Kermanshah, and Harakiri. They have immense supplies

127 "History of 1918 Flu Pandemic." Centers for Disease Control and Prevention. Last modified January 22, 2019.https://www.cdc.gov/flu/pandemic-resources/1918-commemoration/1918-pandemic-history.htm.

of *much-needed medicine, supply of which is almost entirely exhausted in Persia.* Epidemic of influenza prevails and quinine retails at $125 a pound."[128]

In this transcript, the American Relief Commission was charged with supplying Iran specifically with viral medication for the pandemic's relief efforts. The point that is being made here, is that these viral and bacterial outbreaks do happen, and these things will continue to happen. There will be war, there will be sickness, there will be pestilence and famine.[129] People will be injured, and people will lose their lives. It is the way of humanity, as we can see today when we look into our more recent history. It is obvious people know this fact, as panic and fear have driven people nationwide to hoard supplies at grocery and department stores.[130] Shelves are empty. Supply simply cannot keep up with demand.

Was the 1918 Influenza epidemic bad? Sure it was. It certainly wasn't great. It's obvious here by the way the United States, Britain, and Germany have been unleashing their national "wartime powers" not seen since WWI and WWII.[131] And there good

---

128 "The Minister in Persia (Caldwell) to the Secretary of State. Papers Relating to the Foreign Relations of the United States, 1918, Supplement 2, The World War." Office of the Historian. Last modified October 2, 1918.https://history.state.gov/historicaldocuments/frus1918Supp02/d709.

129 "African Locust Swarm Headed for Middle East." Worthy Christian News. Last modified March 17, 2020.https://www.worthynews.com/47840-african-locust-swarm-headed-for-middle-east.

130 Rawlinson, Kevin. "'This Enemy Can Be Deadly': Boris Johnson Invokes Wartime Language." The Guardian. Last modified March 18, 2020.https://www.theguardian.com/world/2020/mar/17/enemy-deadly-boris-johnson-invokes-wartime-language-coronavirus.

131 "Trump Says He Will Invoke Wartime Act to Fight 'enemy' Coronavirus." U.S. Last modified March 19, 2020.https://www.reuters.com/article/us-health-coronavirus-usa-trump-act/trump-says-he-will-invoke-wartime-act-to-fight-enemy-coronavirus-idUSKBN2152XL?feedType=RSS&feedName=domesticNews.

reason to be aware to the history behind this whole "Pandemic" feature of post-Modern America. With the United Nations and WHO taking aim at uniting countries across the globe to fight CoVID-19 in unity and paralleled coordination, it should make you ponder the political freedom's that everybody has taken for granted here at home. I feel as of right now our American liberty is being thrown under the bus in some sense. Some might say all for an illusion of a false sense of security.[132] A certain security that absolutely no government can offer you, or your family.

Statistical numbers on fatalities due to this global pandemic just aren't matching up with the reality of this fully overblown response and lock-down of millions upon millions of people across the globe. Here's the breakdown for infections: "COVID-19: Approximately 247,400 cases worldwide; 14,250 cases in the U.S. as of Mar. 20, 2020*. Regular Flu: Estimated 1 billion cases worldwide; 9.3 million to 45 million cases in the U.S. per year. And here's the breakdown for Deaths: COVID-19: Approximately 10,067 deaths reported worldwide; 205 deaths in the U.S., as of Mar. 20, 2020.* And for the regular Flu: 291,000 to 646,000 deaths worldwide; 12,000 to 61,000 deaths in the U.S. per year."[133]

As we all in America sit and wait out what the mainstream media has dubbed the newest pandemic to affect humanity, we should take time to appreciate everything that we have in our own lives. This means educating ourselves on issues that we do not understand. This also means we should also take this time to

132 "COVID-19: Is A Psyop – Cabal Wants To Turn The World Into A Militarized Police State." Investment Watch – Spreading the Truth. Empowering the People. Last modified February 19, 2020.https://www.investmentwatchblog.com/covid-19-is-a-psyop-cabal-wants-to-turn-the-world-into-a-militiarized-police-state/.

133 Dr. Maragakis, LisaL. "Coronavirus Disease 2019 Vs. the Flu." Johns Hopkins Medicine, Based in Baltimore, Maryland. Accessed March 19,2020.https://www.hopkinsmedicine.org/health/conditions-and-diseases/coronavirus/coronavirus-disease-2019-vs-the-flu.

reflect on our own household and community. As we endure our newest and most politically uncharted direction in human history, we should also ponder taking on an old-time responsibility and obligation to our American solidarity, heritage, and traditional acts of participation in community affairs. We have hit a crossroads in humanity's timeline. From here on out, regardless of your social class and occupation, we are all prisoners of the political and social cycle that we as individuals choose (and don't choose) to be part of.

Rejecting Early American Genocide

It was certainly polarizational issues that made the 19th century a true "wild west," and I really find "wild west" fits in every sense of the phrase…

The American Settler's from back east came over the Rocky Mountains with both broken dreams and real optimism for a new successful life. Each miner, settler, businessman (or woman), and government employee had their own personal reasons for leading a new life in California. The financial burden of the 1837 financial collapse was a national hardship all on its own for the soon-to-be Settler headed out west.[134] American Economist Martin Armstrong wrote, "The U.S. entered a serious economic depression following the failure of the New Orleans cotton brokerage firm, Herman Briggs & Co in March of 1837. Inflated land values, speculation and wildcat banking contributed to the crisis, which became known as the "Hard Times of 1837-1843." New York banks suspended payments in gold on May 10th and

134 Smith, Daniel L. "New American Settlers." In 1845-1870 An Untold Story of Northern California: The American Settler's First Documented Accounts of their Unwelcome Arrival, 20. Publication Consultants, 2019. Print.

financial panic ensued. At least 800 US banks suspended payment in gold and 618 banks failed before the year was out."[135]

With the discovery of gold in California and the resulting influx of emigrants and immigrants; it seemed almost inevitable that the U.S. government would openly authorize the 1862 Homestead Act. This decree would guarantee all American citizens permanent private ownership of newly acquired territory west of the Mississippi river.[136] Economic growth would boom for the nation given the limitless resources of the newly acquired land.Timber, hunting, fishing, mining, commercial business, and government would take over. It was the principle economic body that California would come to offer a rapidly expanding nation, which was now recovering from a financial meltdown. This new economic and cultural opportunity didn't just benefit the legitimate law-abiding Settlers, but this new world also opened up to the criminal and unprincipled elements of American society as well. A somber reality to the preceding historical events throughout to the mid-19th century.

This same reality applies to the cultural similarities in unprincipled behavior that *both Settlers and Natives exhibited equally between each other*, as both played a part in hostile antagonization. I stand with Michael Medved when the word genocide in no way fits as a description of the treatment of Native Americans by British colonists or, later, American Settlers. Further, in "the 400-year history of American contact with the Indians includes many

135 Armstrong, Martin A. "Panic of 1837." Princeton Economic Institute. Last modified January 12, 2014. https://www.armstrongeconomics.com/panic-of-1837/.

136 "Act of May 20, 1862 (Homestead Act), Public Law 37-64 (12 STAT 392); 5/20/1862; Enrolled Acts and Resolutions of Congress, 1789 - 2011; General Records of the United States Government, Record Group 11; National Archives Building, Washington, DC." DocsTeach, 20 May 1862, www.docsteach.org/documents/document/homestead-act.

examples of white cruelty and viciousness --- just as the Native Americans frequently (indeed, regularly) dealt with the European newcomers with monstrous brutality and, indeed, savagery. In fact, reading the history of the relationship between British settlers and Native Americans it's obvious that the blood-thirsty excesses of one group provoked blood thirsty excesses from the other, in a cycle that listed with scant interruption for several hundred years."[137]

"But none of the warfare (including an Indian attack in 1675 that succeeded in butchering a full one-fourth of the white population of Connecticut and claimed additional thousands of casualties throughout New England) on either side amounted to genocide. Colonial and, later, the American government, never endorsed or practiced a policy of Indian extermination; rather, the official leaders of white society tried to restrain some of their settlers and militias and paramilitary groups from unnecessary conflict and brutality. Moreover, the real decimation of Indian populations had nothing to do with massacres or military actions, but rather stemmed from infectious diseases that white settlers brought with them at the time they first arrived in the New World."[138]

UCLA professor Jared Diamond, author of the acclaimed bestseller "Guns, Germs, and Steel: The Fates of Human Societies," writes:

"Throughout the Americas, diseases introduced with Europeans spread from tribe to tribe far in advance of the Europeans themselves, killing an estimated 95 percent of the pre-Colombian Native American population. The most populous and highly organized native societies of North America, the Mississippian chiefdom's, disappeared in that way between 1492

137 Medved, Michael. "Reject the Lie of White "Genocide" Against Native Americans." Townhall. Last modified September 19, 2007. https://townhall.com/columnists/michaelmedved/2007/09/19/reject-the-lie-of-white-genocide-against-native-americans-n989275.

138 Medved.

and the late 1600's, even before Europeans themselves made their first settlement on the Mississippi River (page 78). The main killers were Old World germs to which Indians had never been exposed, and against which they therefore had neither immune nor genetic resistance. Smallpox, measles, influenza, and typhus rank top among the killers." (page 212). As for the most advanced native societies of North America, those of the U.S. Southeast and the Mississippi River system, their destruction was accomplished largely by germs alone, introduced by early European explorers and advancing ahead of them" (page 374)."

Obviously, the decimation of native population by European germs represents an enormous tragedy, but in no sense does it represent a crime. Stories of deliberate infection by passing along "small-pox blankets" are based exclusively on two letters from British soldiers in 1763, at the end of the bitter and bloody French and Indian War. By that time, Indian populations (including those in the area) had already been terribly impacted by smallpox, and there's no evidence of a particularly devastating outbreak as a result of British policy. Medved writes, "For the most part, Indians were infected by devastating diseases even before they made direct contact with Europeans: other Indians who had already been exposed to the germs, carried them with them to virtually every corner of North America and many British explorers and settlers found empty, abandoned villages (as did the Pilgrims) and greatly reduced populations when they first arrived."[139]

As Medved has said, "*Sympathy for Native Americans and admiration for their cultures in no way requires a belief in European or American genocide.*" Jared Diamond›s book (and countless others) makes clear, the mass migration of Europeans to the New World and the rapid displacement and replacement of Native populations is hardly a unique interchange in human history. On

139 Medved.

six continents, such shifting populations – with countless cruel invasions and occupations and social destructions and replacements - have been the rule rather than the exception.

I have found a lot of evidence difficult to obtain through large institutions bureaucratic archives. These are crucial for a more thorough and explicit observation on specific events that had occurred in relationship to the unprincipled behaviors and actions of those few individuals or groups. Some of this evidence that I have been able to successfully retrieve truly illustrate this particular viewpoint. Is this finally a small beam of light on the topic of relational nuances that occurred on both sides of the cultural aisle? *The truth of the matter* is that all of the overall regional hostility came down to certain specific cultural customs or traditions, which also included the erosion (or complete absence) *of any personal ethical and moral values.*

This information is a rigid "shock-and-awe" to the individuals not necessarily awake to the "woke narrative" and still intellectually drowning in today's public school and social-media propaganda. The notion that unique viciousness to Native Americans represents our "original sin" fails to put European contact with these struggling Stone Age societies in any context whatsoever, and only serves the purposes of those who want to foster inappropriate guilt, uncertainty, and shame in all Americans ignorant of the facts.

Finally, a nation ashamed of its past will fear its future. "One of the most urgent needs in culture and education for the United States of America is discarding the stupid, groundless and anti-American lies that characterize contemporary political correctness. The right place to begin is to confront, resist and reject the all-too-common line that our rightly admired forebears involved themselves in genocide. The early colonists and settlers can hardly qualify as perfect but describing them in Hitlerian, mass-murdering terms represents an act of brain-dead defamation."[140]

---

140 Medved.

THE ATLANTIC SLAVE TRADE & POOR WHITE PEOPLE

Poor white people. It's an interestingly good topic. It never gets brought up. About one-third of the cotton-belt's white population did not own land or slaves. I guess this is why it's important to understand more about how this particular selection of people in this particular region identified with their status and place in society.

The Panic of 1837 was a financial collapse reminiscent of Wall Street's plunge in our more contemporary times. It utterly destroyed everything associated with finances, and the lower classes would take the brunt of the early-American financial collapse. Even small-time farmers and landholders found themselves quickly stripped of their earnings, and savings.

Throughout the 1840's, biting at the ankle of the recession, almost one million slaves spilled into the deep south. The economic displacement for unskilled and partly skilled white laborers was overwhelming. Plantation slavery made any sort of white labor completely unnecessary—of course unless it was to fill a serious labor need—like during the planting and harvesting seasons specifically (kind of like Walmart at Christmas). Unemployment and underemployment were extremely high with long periods of time in between. Economic consequences for these poor whites were a certain part of the fallout of living in a slave society, although daily violence, mistreatment, and humiliations were behaviors they were not subjected too.

Even when these poor whites increasingly shifted their labors towards work that did not involve agriculture, the deep south could not afford the full employment. Daily and seasonal labor was the only typical work available, and even then, it left many people without work for most parts of the year. Many white laborer's found work that had them traveling long distances—this would cause them to completely leave their families and belongings behind. This was just for short term work! In the South, the more available jobs to take were the most dangerous. Digging ditches for agricultural aqueducts, or mining—work labeled "too dangerous for Negro property." I think the hardest thing for poor white laborers was the threats of constantly being told that there were thousands of blacks ready to take their place if they choose to ask for better wages or ask for a safer work environment.[141]

141 Richard M. Morris, "The Measure of Bondage in the Slave States," The Mississippi Valley Historical Review 41, No. 2 (Sept. 1954): 223; 228.

In the latter years of the 1850's that a white laborer by the name of Isaac Grimes wrote: "...awful scarce. Couldn't hardly get work [and] wages [were] so low – I have worked that time for $5.00 a month and board. Worked with oxen's, all [I] could get for work." Another white laborer from Georgia mentioned: "... the slaveholders could get the slave for almost nothing and the poor young men like myself, could not get a job."[142] Not only did poor whites possess class awareness to their status in society, but they also became resentfully bitter of slave owners. These poor whites would see their labor made useless. Some of them would even choose to leave the southern antebellum altogether. Some would live off the land, and other would run from the law. Still, others would work the odd job to make their own ends meet.

It was the heavy emphasis on hiring slaves throughout the 1840's and 1850's that compounded on class troubles. As poor whites moved into the large southern cities from rural areas, racial tensions continued to mount. It was to no surprise that poor class whites became upset, and even at times hostile, about their positioning in the southern economy. As a result of their class awareness, they would threaten to leave slave politics altogether. They would make their points heard about the viability of the institution of slavery and how necessary support from the working poor class citizens made that stability happen. Ultimately, they made their unhappiness to the upper classes known. A great example of this aforementioned issue: White laborers protested and made a call to action stating, "the suppression of the abuses committed by the owners of negro mechanics in 'permitting their slaves to go at large, trade as free men, [and] hire themselves out'...

142 Colleen M. Elliot and Louise A. Moxley, eds. The Tennessee Civil War Veterans Questionnaires, Vols. 1-5. (Easley, SC: Southern Historical Press, Inc., 1985), Vol. 3, 966; Vol. 3, 1057.

to the...direct injury of the mechanical classes in open violation of social right."

Even R. H. Purdom would give a stark warning: "early, decided course for the speedy suppression of the intolerable abuses" taken on by white workers was absolutely necessary for the "permanent welfare of the institution of slavery itself."[143] Mr. Purdom was a master mechanic who stood up to address a meeting in Jackson, Mississippi gave a stark warning to the elite's controlling the southern economy. It was by this point that even the poor working white class were ready to turn coat on their own institutions—and their own people.

This event proves that the ancient institution of slavery, which had been broken by Moses and the Israelite's from Egypt as commanded by God, was an unstable and nonviable solution from the beginning of its contemporary conception. George Mason of Virginia, a representative who championed abolition mentioned, "Every master of slaves is born a petty tyrant. They bring the judgment of heaven upon a country. As nations cannot be rewarded or punished in the next world, they must be in this. By an inevitable chain of causes and effects, Providence punishes national sins by national calamities."[144]

...the poor whites of early-America were well aware of their "social status".

143 "Mechanical Association," Mississippian State Gazette, Dec. 29, 1858, 3.

144 Beliles, Mark A., and Stephen K. McDowell. "The War for the Union." In America's Providential History, 3rd ed., 227. Charlottesville: Providence Foundation, 1989.

Medieval Jesters – And Their Parallels in Modern America

Jesters were a key part of many Medieval courts. But are Jesters still among us?

The Jester was common in the times of castles, villages, chainmail, and treachery. In Medieval Europe,the elites and nobility would hire jesters in which the aristocratic family would regard them as "mascots". These characters were well-educated individuals who came from a variety of diverse upbringings. Jesters are known for their crazy styles and abstract apparel.[145] All of this for the attention of the court of course, and sometime the humility. These people were hired to amuse the lord and the lord's guests. At times, Jesters, oddly enough, were paid to criticize themtoo!

These people of humor and talents had a privilege given to them by their master: freedom of speech. Interestingly enough, Jesters were one of the few people in their lord's presence that could speak their minds freely without risk of punishment. They typically used humor and parody to joke around and "razz" the nobles and elites.[146] Bringing bad news was another job for the Jester to deliver to their master - when paid appropriately.

Types of Jester

Excessive misbehavior though, would result in some form of harsh punishment. There were two primary types of Jesters in Medieval Europe – the *natural fool* and the*licensed fool.* The natural fool was known as moronic in social setting; whereas the licensed fool had the legal privileges granted to them to avoid the mentioned court punishments for bad behavior.

The most apparent description of the Jester is a person who worked under the employment of a European noble, telling jokes and providing entertainment. Bright colors with eccentric hats and bells were a calling card for Jesters. A couple of surprising details pertaining to symbolism are the hat and scepter that Jesters often wore and carried. There was a head usually carved into the top of the scepter, representing the actor. The scepter was more

145 Billington, Sandra. "*A Social History of the Fool,*" The Harvester Press, 1984. ISBN 0-7108-0610-8

146 Doran, John. "*A History of Court Fools,*" 1858.

or less ornamental and it was called a "marotte".[147] This staff was symbolic in representing the authority of the royal court.

Overall, many of these actors held small roles in the courts they worked for (or were pressed into) and livened up most social events. It was some serious responsibility and even obligation for the Jester to bring a smile to a sick or often angry King or Monarch. This position was one held purely for the amusement and humor of his master. Assisting in preventing state affairs from becoming too serious was a main priority to the Jester, as well as bringing excitement to courtly meals, apparently to help assist in aiding with digestion.

HOW THE JESTER IS PORTRAYED TODAY

Most of the Jester's entertainment in the courts or within the master's domain would likely include music (vocal and with an instrument), prop and physical comedy, storytelling and myth bringing. Some historians also suggest that some Jesters juggled and were acrobatic. Basic tools, props, and instruments were all that was necessary for performances in the court.[148]

Jesters are comparable to today's clowns. They also parallel Hollywood actors and musical artists. Today's artists essentially do the same job as the Jester of the feudalistic courts. The only difference is artists are able to connect to mass audience, whereas the Jester could only reach the royal courts and social gatherings. I mean – the printing press didn't even arrive until the 15th century!

Indeed, there are a number of similarities between Jesters and modern-day entertainment. For example, soap opera characters are sometimes corporate people working against one another's rivals

147 Hyers, M. Conrad, "*The Spirituality of Comedy: Comic Heroism in a Tragic World.*"1996 Transaction Publishers ISBN 1-56000-218-2

148 Otto, Beatrice K.,"*Fools Are Everywhere: The Court Jester Around the World,* "Chicago University Press, 2001

and family members. This could be because some Hollywood entertainment is produced and designed to be geared towards the elites and higher classes of American society. Again, this mimics the Jester entertaining the master and getting paid for it.[149]

It is the same today in modern America, just as the elites and nobility would have done behind castle walls. Today, actors are hired in Hollywood, and some powerful people could consider them as "mascots". Theseactors, actresses, and musicians todayare typically well-educated individuals who come from a variation of diverse upbringings – just as the Jesters of the past.

Actors, actresses, and musicians today are known for their crazy styles and abstract apparel – just as the Jesters of the past. All of this for the constant need for attention from the audience at home – just as Jesters would in court of course.

Actors, actresses, and musicians today are people who are hired to amuse the master (the elite) and the master's guests (the voters) – just as the Jesters of the past.And finally, at times, Jesters were paid to criticize the nobility at court…[150] Just like the actors, actresses, and musicians today in Hollywood who are using television and radio for their political and social arguments using their platforms… which is something that you would not find from Jesters of the Royal Courts for fear of cruel punishment.

Jesters are not a thing of the past. They are here today.

---

149 Southworth, John, *Fools and Jesters at the English Court,* Sutton Publishing, 1998. ISBN 0-7509-1773-3

150 Welsford, Enid: "*The Fool: His Social and Literary History*" (out of print) (1935 + subsequent reprints): ISBN 1-299-14274-5

California in the American Civil War

California is not talked about too much in the context of the American Civil War (1861-65). It had only joined the Union in 1850 and was far from the main action in the east of the USA. However, California did have a part to play during the US Civil War.

California and Statehood

It was prior to 1850 that the true nature of the Wild West existed in California, this pristine region of the country. Ideology was split, and even within the split, there was further fracturing due to cultural differences as well as consistent fighting for property rights. The discovery of gold exacerbated the issue of regional turmoil as California was pulled into the US Civil War. This is just the tip of the iceberg on how California existed during this era. Many, or almost all people, are not aware of how truly important California as a region was during the Civil War.

California and Californians themselves endured in its struggle and existence. California had essentially wrapped itself in the American Civil War in politics, finances, and culture. California ethos (or ideology) was absolutely split politically. In hindsight, it was seemingly more than "Blue & Grey" ideology in a state that was overwhelmingly Native American. California had always been home to a Native American and slave population well before being "settled" by Americans East of the Mississippi.

It all started when California made statehood in 1850. Soon thereafter in 1859, the legislature of California was split into two states – Northern California and Southern California (as Colorado Territory). Even though Southern California was part of the Union, it had strong Confederate sympathies. These Confederate ties were due to the large number of Southerners who had transplanted to the Southern California area during the famous Gold Rush. This mass-relocation showed its evidence in the 1860 presidential elections. Lincoln had received only 25% of the Los Angeles vote.

On the brink of the Civil War California chose the Union, abandoning three other choices: secession, neutrality, and independence.

Arguments and counterarguments were made from every political and civic level of the community. It seemed as though some people were in doubt and tossed about in which decision it should have been. Although California was isolated from the conflict in the East and despite the diversified political beliefs of her people, a feeling of loyalty to the United States and federal government was overwhelming. California Republican and Union-Democratic leaders expressed an unwavering loyalty in a multitude of ways.

Ultimately, the Unionist political candidates took over two-thirds of the votes for state government. Various estimates have been guessed regarding the number of pro-Confederates in the population in California. Indeed, although the loyalty of the state appeared evident, militias were activated.

REVENUE AND TURMOIL

Oaths of loyalty were required for certain groups and individuals, and of course occasional military arrests were made to solidify loyalty. Regardless, California would end up being a major financial contributor to the federal government during the Civil War, because the gold deposits were direct revenue to pay for war costs. In fact, quite a large portion of the federal government's war budget was reinforced by new gold from California's Sierra Nevada mountain range. General Grant, in fact, said, "I do not know what we could do in this great national emergency, were it not for the gold sent from California."

The U.S Army built and operated many fortifications along frontier trails in the Sierra Nevada mountain range in California. What people do not know is that although California leaned towards the Union, they were so wrapped up in their own civil discord at home they were not able to send organized regiments east. In late 1861, a Confederate Brigadier General Henry Sibley was allowed to open up an easier route into California through northern Arizona Territory, with further instruction to capture the gold fields in San Francisco by Confederate President Jefferson Davis. This instruction would be for the purpose of a preemptive strike against the Unionist state and in turn show how significant California really was in the Civil War.

Little did both sides realize, California was in regional turmoil on its own accord without the help of a formal war. Now, aside from the status quo bleeding "Blue & Grey," some non-traditional elements to the war are that the settlers who had come to California were still dealing with the effects of settling tribal lands, adding negative social, criminal, and economic dilemmas between the local Native American tribes, settlers, and the U.S. government.[151] For example, in Humboldt County (approximately 271 miles north of San Francisco) on March 29, 1862, a Humboldt Times headline read, *"Horrible Indian Outrages!—The Savages Become Bolder!"*

In this letter submitted to the paper's editors on March 27, 1862, the citizens of Arcata were "really alarmed at the extent of their (the Native America) evil deeds and the increased boldness and daring… ". The letter states that local natives shot Mr. Zehendner and burned his home, burnt Goodman's house and the next day, Mrs. Brehmer's. On Friday, March 28, Augustus Bates was shot and killed. The natives burned his house. The letter ends, "What a sudden reverse - peace and fancied security one day - death and destruction the next. Surely human life is mutable and occurrences like this bring the fact impressively to our mind. This is a gloomy letter, and ours is a gloomy town. I can think and write of nothing else."

151 Charles B. Turrill. *"San Francisco and the Civil War."* Museum of the City of San Francisco. Last modified 1876. http://www.sfmuseum.org/hist5/civwar.html.

STILL THE WILD WEST

On April 2, 1862, many of the citizens of Arcata signed a petition asking the military to remove all the Native Americans from the county completely and push them far away. They went on to state that they didn't want them in Mendocino County or Crescent City – as it was too easy to get back.[152]This shows that California was essentially dealing with its own problems, as well as the internal war. With a combination of civic non-cohesion of indigenous native populations, the settlers of the newly established towns, and with the two warring governments remaining active in the state, it appears as though both the centralized governments failed to see the deeper issue residing in California.[153]

Overall, there were handfuls of land skirmishes in California. Within the timeline of the war, California seemed to be most concerned with keeping political tension at a minimum. A further example of the civil issues that California would have to navigate would be the Bullion Bend Robbery. Two stagecoaches were robbed of their silver and gold near Placerville. A letter was left for authorities explaining that they were not committed criminals but carrying out a subversive operation to funnel money to the Confederacy.[154]

In 1864, a magistrate and handful of men became known as the Partisan Rangers. They sacked the property of Union-loyal civilians in the rural and outlying areas around Stockton. For the next two years they posed as "Confederate Partisan Rangers" but acted out criminally. They were found committing robberies, thefts, and murders located in the counties of San Joaquin Valley,

---

152 "Horrible Indian Outrages! - The Savages Become Bolder!" *The Humboldt Times*, March 29th, 1862. p.3 col. 1.

153 Brian McGinty. "I Will Call a Traitor a Traitor: Albert Sidney Johnston." Civil War Times Illustrated, 1981.

154 John Boessenecker (1993).*Badge and Buckshot: Lawlessness in Old California.* Norman: University of Oklahoma Press. pp. 133–157. ISBN 0806125101. Retrieved 21 October 2018.

Santa Cruz, Monterey, Santa Clara, and a few other counties located in Southern California.[155]

A final notable incident required a superb show of force by the Federal Cavalry in the streets of San Bernardino at the end of election day in September of 1864. They quelled a Confederate political demonstration during the gubernatorial elections in San Bernardino County.[156]

California's Permanent Divide

After the Civil War ended in California the state took greater control and quickly began to integrate the counties of what would end up being on today's political boundary maps. With the last of the Pacific coast Native Americans being rounded up to be placed on reservations and the fizzling out of what would come to be known as Westward Expansion, the state would start to consolidate its power as the new and now truly established authority in the West.[157]

It was now no longer considered the Wild West – as you would see on old black and white Western movies. Even so, the Union won the Civil War and California adopted the Union's policies, politically--there would always be a permanently heavy Democratic and Republican divide that would simmer beneath the voting cracks.

---

155 William B. Secrest, (2007). *California Badmen: Mean Men with Guns.* Sanger, Calif.: Word Dancer Press. pp. 143–147. ISBN 1884995519. Retrieved 21 October 2018.

156 Henry Martyn Lazelle; Leslie J. Perry (1897*). The War of the Rebellion: A Compilation of the Official Records of the Union and Confederate Armies.* U.S. Government Printing Office. Retrieved 21 October 2018.

157 Kevin Starr. *California: A History.* New York: Modern Library, 2015

A Modern Renaissance Long Gone

There has been an undertaking by individuals and institutions, with an anti-American philosophy to life, seeking to destroy traditional American culture. I have written about the dangers lurking behind rewriting traditional national history to fit the needs of a certain anti-American political agenda. It's absolutely maddening in apparent obviousness how people are "propping up" false teachers. They use these people as pawns to push deviant propaganda that's meant to serve nobody in our society with any sustainable good. Lately, it's only serving wants, hopelessness, and hate.

In fact, the rewrite of history (think,1619 Project)is meant to meet an organizational agenda that pushes Marxist, communist, socialist, and… wait for it… tribalistic mentalities.[158] History is not something that can be re-written. History is foundational. Events that had occurred, are occurring, and that will occur, are all true events. This is what makes history foundational. The historical side of life has lost its value, to the most extreme degree.

158 "Historians Debunk the 1619 Project." TheTrumpet.com. Accessed May8,2021. https://www.thetrumpet.com/21771-historians-debunk-the-1619-project.

Statues being toppled, U.S. tradition shredded (think the U.S. Constitution and her principles), history being re-written in complete fallacy.[159] So it's all looking to be an evil plot that meets the needs to an end. We all know what the end *is,* the question is, do we acknowledge it?

Whatever the end may be (I leave that up to the reader to come to that conclusion), it's an ending that leaves what we used to know as "options" in life, has now been limited. Awhile back ago, I was in a discussion with a friend over the direction of the United States as we know it. He brought up how "we need a Renaissance in America." I politely suggested to him that we had already had one. Not the renaissance that was experienced in the 16thand 17thcenturies.

On the contrary, I was talking about our *modern cultural Renaissance* experienced from the 1950's to a little after the break of the new millennium in the United States. I am not saying that the "cultural revolution" was anything to be happy about, in fact, it downright trashed our founding principles and drug them through the mud. However, with such excesses of unchecked freedom that brings our society down, comes the good that God pulls from the bad that occurs.

For instance, with all the cultural trash that was bred out of the 1960's to the millennium, you have got to be impressed with the technological advances our nation has made. You can't thank anything else but that fine balance of liberty and freedom that we are afforded here in our nation. It's what makes these societal advances even possible. For that, we can all be thankful for the instant comfort and gratification that liberal society worships. There is always a fine line balance between holding back

159 Scully, Rachel, and James Bikales. "A List of the Statues Across the US Toppled, Vandalized or Officially Removed Amid Protests." TheHill. Last modified June 17, 2020. https://thehill.com/homenews/state-watch/502492-list-statues-toppled-vandalized-removed-protests.

and excessive behavior (I recommend reading,*An All-Consuming Century*by Gary S. Cross).

The internet was the lifeblood of the advancement of this modern renaissance when it was discovered and then commercialized. It was in the early 1990s that America Online and that annoying 3-minute connection garble started it all. We all remember that. Nintendo. Computers. Gaming. Social Media. Chat Rooms. Websites. Communication was not only born in our modern renaissance, but it was this technology that enabled the growth of extremes and it's resulting deviant behaviors that only now people are beginning to acknowledge (if not aware already) in American homes everywhere.

Our modern Renaissance ended somewhere in the late-2000's. Everything now in our modern culture is just downright rehashed. Everything that is culturally presented is digested, thrown-up, and then painted back onto a white canvass for another presentation. It's disgusting. Look what has become of it. All in the name of politics that had not been finished at the end of the first American Civil War.

I mean, what do you expect whenPresident Johnson's 1865 proclamationmoved to pardon the entirety of those Democratic leaders on the Confederate side who*should have been*fully prosecuted and then executed for their treason against God, Country, and*The People.*[160] Instead, we allowed them back into government without any formal prosecution. Look around you today, and you should see the consequences of this poor political decision on behalf of the Union in 1865.

So…

Here we are today. History shredded and rewritten proves a picture-perfect result of a lack of education, lack of sensitization,

160 "President Johnson's Amnesty Proclamation; Restoration to Rights of Property Except in Slaves." The New York Times. Last modified May 30, 1865. https://www.nytimes.com/1865/05/30/archives/president-johnsons-amnesty-proclamation-restoration-to-rights-of.html.

lack of logic, lack of self-worth, and where a lack of spiritual truth gets you. A board room full of liberal "intellectuals" making up "new history" like it's a Dungeons and Dragons board game, that places the blame on America's Founders for why our nation got this way. They refuse to take the blame for their own self-destructive cultural habits that by all rights should get them locked away. We all wake-up and live life with the same basic components. Some of us Americans just choose to put actual effort into trying to change this nation, and life in general, for the betterment of *The People* and not just a few groups of people.

It's really about the truth in principle.

A Brief and Quite Serious Conclusion

The fact of the matter is this. Our once splendorous world we were gifted at Creation, including our own nation, is the RMS Titanic going under. This was at a once steady pace. We all became numb to the truth in understanding because we were manipulated. We were once Americans who strived for the "E" in excellence. Those who work in the shadows with endless resources played our rightfully earned American nationalism against us.

Those who work to empower themselves through illogical reasoning and political unrestraint to accomplish their ends are responsible for the American fracture that we now call post-Modern America. Since the ship has started to split apart, many Americans are desperately searching for the answers in life to form their own logical conclusions. The issue here then is this: How *do* we form our own conclusions when the information is controlled by government institution?

The answer to this is relatively simple. Keep seeking the truth and follow what *is* logical. The Founding Fathers were relentless in their faith in Jesus Christ. They knew in their hearts that God had providentially guided those truest Christian faithful to *His* promised land. God would never allow *His* "beacon of light" that is North America, to remain a pagan landscape—completely aware of its rejection of our true God. He would use those most foundational to *His Word* to allow the planting and reaping of the seed we call Christianity.

It really is this fundamental *truth* that we adhere too, in Christ, from a pastor's sermon to home Bible study, to the full application of Biblical Scripture throughout our daily lives. You should now see how this nation gifted to us by God, designed under the inspiration of God, could be violently swayed, and destroyed under an ideology of those pushing against traditional American values. It's black and white. It's clear as day. It's not normal.

History is complex. In fact, it's complex America! And as now you can see there's much more to the story than you've ever been told. Now, what you do with this information is something else much different. Since your mind is politically and culturally "reseated," maybe it's about time to start taking another direction in life? Because it's always about dropping the walls and fearlessly taking on a society that has been framed (as of the 1900s) to confuse us and keep us all down in many different ways. We are all on the same ship. There is hope.

Let's sing it off with the hit American 1967 rock band, Buffalo Springfield:

"There's something happening here… What it is ain't exactly clear…"

"There's a man with a gun over there… Telling me I got to beware…"

"I think it's time we stop, children, what's that sound, Everybody look what's going down…"

"There's battle lines being drawn… Nobody's right if everybody's wrong…"

www.ingramcontent.com/pod-product-compliance
Lightning Source LLC
LaVergne TN
LVHW050643100826
845148LV00011B/1962

* 9 7 8 1 6 3 7 4 7 0 4 1 1 *